Bicycling
MAGAZINE'S
1,000
ALL-TIME BEST TIPS
>FULLY REVISED AND UPDATED

RODALE
LIVE YOUR WHOLE LIFE™

Every day our brands connect with and inspire millions of people to live a life of the mind, body, spirit — a whole life.

D0092816

>FULLY REVISED AND UPDATED

Bicycling
MAGAZINE'S

Top Riders Share Their
Secrets to Maximize Fun,
Safety, and Performance

1,000
ALL-TIME BEST TIPS

EDITED BY **BEN HEWITT**

RODALE

Notice

The information in this book is meant to supplement, not replace, proper road cycling and mountain biking training. Like any sport involving speed, equipment, balance, and environmental factors, cycling poses some inherent risk. The editors and publishers advise readers to take full responsibility for their safety and know their limits. Before practicing the skills described in this book, be sure that your equipment is well maintained, and do not take risks beyond your experience, aptitude, training, and comfort level. Mention of specific companies, organizations, or authorities in this book does not imply endorsement by the publisher, nor does mention of specific companies, organizations, or authorities imply that they endorse this book.
Internet addresses and telephone numbers given in this book were accurate at the time it went to press.

CONTENTS

INTRODUCTION

To be a better cyclist, all you really need to do is ride. In fact, that's one of the great beauties of the sport. Every time you turn the pedals, every time you dodge a pothole or rock or root, you're becoming a better cyclist and having fun along the way.

But that's not to say you can't use some help. That's what this book is all about. On the following pages, you'll find 1,000 ways to improve your cycling, tips and tricks coaxed from dozens of the world's top cyclists. Whether you're a roadie, a mountain biker, a long haul tourist, or a weekend-run-to-the-coffee-shop sort of rider, there's a tip (and probably a lot more than one!) for you.

Read, then ride. And then ride some more.

1

23 TIPS FOR SAFETY IN TRAFFIC

Cycling is one of the world's safest and most enjoyable forms of transportation (factor in the health benefits, and it might even come out on top). But there's no denying that 2 tons' worth of sport utility vehicle is something to reckon with. Use these techniques to ensure you don't find yourself SUV (Squashed Under Vehicle).

1. If drivers can't see you, they can't avoid you. That means wearing bright colors (think red, orange, yellow, and white) during daylight hours and equipping your bike with front and rear lights after dusk (or before dawn, if you're the ambitious sort).

2. Ride defensively, but not timidly. You are entitled to a place on the road; use it. Be predictable, and go about your business with a self-assurance that shows you know what you're doing. This helps motorists anticipate your actions and feel comfortable sharing the road with you.

3. Ride well into the lane when traffic is stop-and-go. A cyclist can usually move as fast as—or faster than—cars in heavy traffic, so don't hug the curb, where you're less visible and drivers will be tempted to squeeze by.

4. Stay far enough in the traffic lane to avoid being struck by doors suddenly opening on parked cars. You'll likely hear some honks from following motorists who don't understand why you won't pull to the right to let them pass, but hold your ground. A honk in your ear hurts less than a door in your face, and an opportunity to move right will come soon enough.

(continued on page 4)

NO-EXCUSES BIKE COMMUTING

There's the money you'll save on gas, train fare, and parking. There's the endorphin buzz that will put you in the perfect frame of mind to tackle the workday. There are the environmental benefits. And there's the fitness you'll gain. These are just a few of many benefits of commuting by bicycle. And yet many riders see commuting as some radical undertaking better left to hard-core environmentalists and those unlucky enough to live without internal combustion. Don't let yourself fall victim: If you live within 10 miles or so of your workplace (and most of you do), there's little excuse not to commute by bicycle. Still not convinced? Read on for commonsense solutions to popular commuting excuses.

1. **Excuse:** It's not safe to ride in rush-hour traffic. **Solution:** It's usually possible to get from home to work on less congested backstreets or secondary roads. You may have to ride a few extra minutes, but they will bring you more exercise and enjoyment.

2. **Excuse:** I can't afford a special commuter bike. **Solution:** Use your present bike, or buy a used "beater." Weight is not as much a factor as reliability. An old rigid mountain bike, or a road or hybrid bike with sufficient clearance between the stays and fork blades for wider tires, is ideal for riding city streets.

3. **Excuse:** I have to dress nicely for work and can't stuff my good clothes into panniers. **Solution:** Drive to work one day each week, leave a week's worth of clean clothes, and take the dirty stuff home.

4. **Excuse:** I don't have a place to shower after arriving. **Solution:** To clean up, use a deodorant soap and washcloth at the restroom sink. Or douse a washcloth with rubbing alcohol and wipe yourself down. This cools your body while killing odor-causing germs.

5. **Excuse:** There's no secure place to park my bike. **Solution:** It may not seem so, but check for a storage closet or an out-of-

the-way corner somewhere, like a furnace room. Or stash it with an acquaintance who lives nearby, at a bike shop, or at another business nearby that accommodates cyclists.

6. **Excuse:** I like to sleep, and I'd have to get up earlier if I rode my bike. **Solution:** An extra few minutes of sleep aren't nearly as refreshing as a brisk morning ride. And your evening ride home will leave you relaxed, so you'll sleep more soundly. Quality over quantity.

7. **Excuse:** Due to my work schedule, I'd have to ride in the dark. **Solution:** Wear light-colored, reflective clothing, attach lights and reflectors, and use a route that's lit by streetlights. Reflective safety vests are cheap and stash easily in a pocket.

8. **Excuse:** I don't like riding in the cold/rain/snow. **Solution:** When it's pouring buckets, or sleeting sideways, leave the bike home. But you may start looking forward to your daily rides so much that you invest in a wind jacket, rainwear, tights, mittens, balaclava, booties, thermal socks, and the like. Studded mountain bike tires are available, if you live someplace truly arctic.

9. **Excuse:** My commute is too far to ride. **Solution:** Consider cycling only partway. Drive to within a reasonable distance, park, and ride the rest. Maybe you can even take a bus or train to where your bike is stashed. Look for a well-lit commuter or park-and-ride lot.

10. **Excuse:** I live too close to work to make riding worthwhile. **Solution:** Take a longer, more scenic route either going in or returning home.

11. **Excuse:** People will think I'm weird if I ride a bike to work. **Solution:** They may, but so what? There's a chance that some of them will admire you because you're doing something that's healthful, economical, and protective of the environment and natural resources. Chances are, your good example will cause some of them to give bike commuting a try, too.

5. Don't gain ground at red lights by passing a line of cars on their right. It's illegal, and you can get "doored" from either side. It also irritates motorists because they have to pass you again after the light changes.

6. When you stop for a light, move to the center of your lane. This prevents drivers from edging forward, trapping you between them and the curb. When the light changes, accelerate to your cruising speed before moving right to allow them to pass.

7. Hold a straight line past cars that are intermittently parallel-parked. In other words, don't weave in and out of empty spaces. Drivers might not be ready for you to suddenly reemerge in the traffic lane, and you never know what's hiding in those spaces.

8. Beware of the three most common driver errors that threaten bike riders.

- Turning left in front of an oncoming cyclist who's going straight through an intersection

- Failing to obey a stop sign and pulling in front of a cyclist

- Passing a cyclist and immediately turning right across his or her path

9. If you have the right of way at an intersection, don't coast through, or drivers may assume they can cut in front of you. Keep pedaling, but be prepared to brake.

10. Use your hearing as an early-warning system. Tip-offs to danger include engines revving or slowing, squealing tires, gear changes, and rap music at high volume.

11. Help earn motorists' respect for cyclists by using hand signals for turns, lane changes, and stops. Use your left arm (finger pointed) to signal left turns and braking (palm facing backward with arm at a downward angle). For right turns, hold out your right arm with finger pointed. Forget that business about signaling right turns with the left arm held up. It originated because motorists couldn't reach across to point out the right window.

12. Scan the rear windows of parked cars for someone who might suddenly pull out into your lane or throw open a door. You can also spot a pedestrian who is about to step from between cars.

13. Most potential hazards appear to the front when you're riding through a busy area, so learn to scan each side street and driveway for cars, kids, and pets.

14. When you see a car stopped at a cross street, watch its front wheels. That's the surest way to spot even slight forward movement. If you see any, get ready to brake, swerve, and yell.

15. Forget horns, bells, and whistles as warning devices in traffic. They take too long to use, and most aren't loud enough to be effective. A shout is instant, requires no hands, and gets immediate attention.

16. Resist making an obscene gesture or shouting profanity on the rare occasion that a motorist intentionally harasses you. You may think you're doling out punishment, but psychologists say otherwise. It actually tells the hostile driver that he or she has succeeded, and this encourages more of the same behavior.

17. Likewise, don't meekly pull off the road. Retreating proves that you have been intimidated—another form of reward for the driver. The best response is no response at all. Keep riding as if nothing happened. No good can come from confrontations with hostile operators of large metal boxes. If they don't take it out on you, they might on the next cyclist they see.

18. If a threatening driver gives you the opportunity to get a glimpse of his license plate number, stop and report it to the local law enforcement agency as soon as you see a phone booth. Keep chanting the number to yourself so that you won't forget it.

19. A useful skill in traffic is the "instant turn." This evasive action can prevent an accident when a car passes you and immediately

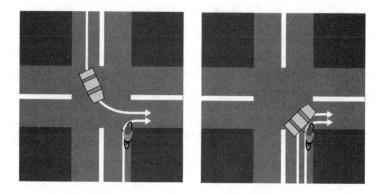

turns right, across your path. It's also useful when an oncoming car turns left in front of you, leaving you no time to brake. To initiate an instant turn, twitch your handlebar to the left to create a lean angle; then immediately dive into a right turn beside the car, avoiding a collision. Practice in your backyard or on the soft surface of the local park.

20. Beware of sun glare, a danger if you ride on busy roads early or late in the day. The low sun makes it difficult for motorists to see a cyclist. Eliminate this risk by altering your route so you don't ride directly into the sun.

21. Use a rearview mirror. Every other type of vehicle has one; don't put yourself at a disadvantage on your bike. A mirror lets you keep a constant check on what's behind without risking potentially dangerous swerves from turning to look back. Mirrors come in many styles that attach to your handlebar, helmet, or glasses.

22. Remember: Just like your car's mirrors, your bike mirror will have blind spots. You must also glance back quickly to double-check before making a lane change or a left turn. A vehicle could be coming up just outside the mirror's field of view.

23. If you've ever wondered how dangerous it is to cycle in a polluted urban area, take a deep breath and relax. A study found that riding a bike in New York City is far less damaging to the lungs than smoking cigarettes or even being in a room full of smokers. In fact, the amount of carbon monoxide in the blood of midtown bike messengers actually declined during the course of a day, prompting speculation that hard breathing may expel pollutants from the lungs.

2 ⟫⟫⟫

35 TIPS FOR PERFECT RIDING POSITIONS

L ance Armstrong knows. So does Jan Ullrich. And Tyler Hamilton. What do these famous professional racers know? That proper fit is paramount. And that's true whether you're gunning for the Tour de France or your local Tour de Coffee Shop. Fact is, an ill-fitting bike is an invitation to pain, frustration, and poor performance. Remember: Your ideal riding position results from adjusting your bike to fit your body, not the other way 'round. Use these tips to dial your fit and become more comfortable (and maybe even faster) on your bike.

Road Bike

1. Avoid road rider's rigor mortis. Keep your elbows bent and relaxed, to absorb shock and prevent veering if you hit a bump. Paradoxically, the more relaxed you are, the more quickly you'll be able to react to hazards.

2. Keep your arms in line with your body, not splayed to the side, to make a more compact, aerodynamic package.

3. Most neophyte roadies experience upper-body muscle soreness. The operative words: Be still. Imagine the calories burned by rocking from side to side with every pedal stroke on a 25-mile ride. Wouldn't you rather use that energy to pedal faster or farther (or—what the heck—both)?

4. Beware of creeping forward on the saddle and hunching your back when you're tired. Shift to a higher gear and stand to pedal periodically, to prevent stiffness in your hips and back.

5. Avoid putting your head down, especially when you're tired. For safety's sake, keep your eyes on what's coming, looking as far up the road as is comfortable. Periodically tilt your head from side to side to stretch and relax your neck muscles.

6. Relax your grip. On smooth, traffic-free pavement, practice draping your hands over the handlebar. Not only will this help alleviate muscle tension; it will reduce the amount of numbing road vibration that's transmitted to your body.

7. Change hand positions frequently. Grasp the drops for descents or high-speed riding, and the brake lever hoods for relaxed cruising. On long climbs, hold the top of the bar to sit upright and open your chest for easier breathing. When standing, grasp the hoods lightly, and gently rock the bike from side to side in sync with your pedal strokes. Always keep each thumb and a finger closed around the hood or bar to prevent yourself from losing hold on an unexpected bump.

8. Handlebar width should equal shoulder width. Err on the side of a wider bar to open your chest for breathing. Some models are available with a large drop (vertical distance) to help big hands fit into the hooks. Position the bottom, flat portion of the bar horizontally or pointed slightly down toward the rear hub.

9. Brake levers can be moved around the curve of the bar to give you the best compromise between holding the hoods and braking when your hands are in the bar drops. Experiment with different positions, starting with the lever hoods level with the handlebar top.

10. Position your stem so that the top of your handlebar is about an inch below the top of your saddle. Aspiring racers may want a slightly lower position for aerodynamics, while touring cyclists might opt for a more upright posture. As always, listen to your body and adjust your bike accordingly.

11. The combined dimensions of top tube and stem length, which determine your "reach," vary according to your flexibility and anatomy. While there is no ultimate prescription, spend whatever time and money it takes to find the right mix because this measurement, more than anything else, will dictate your level of comfort. A good starting point: When you're comfortably seated with elbows slightly bent and hands on the brake hoods, the front hub should be obscured by the handlebar. This is a relatively upright position. With time you may benefit from a longer stem

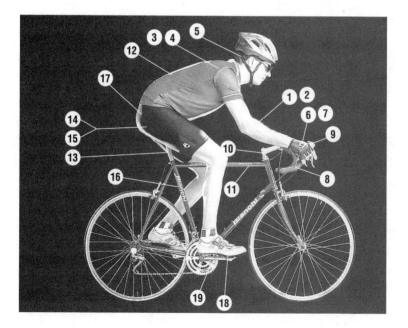

(continued on page 12)

MORE POSITION POINTERS

1. Compared with a man of the same height, a woman generally needs a bike that measures about 2 centimeters less between the seat tube and the head tube. This is because women typically have shorter torsos, requiring less reach to the handlebar. Look for a manufacturer that makes woman-specific frames; there are many of them.

2. Hybrids generally have 700C wheels like a road bike, but a flat handlebar like a mountain bike. They are close to road bikes for most dimensions. However, for greater crotch clearance, you may wish to select a frame size at the small end of your acceptable range if you'll be riding it off-road. Some hybrids also have a higher bottom bracket than road bikes, which means their stand-over height will be less for the identical size frame. Strive for at least 2 inches of clearance between your crotch and the top tube.

3. Many hybrids come with a short, high-rise stem, supplying an upright position for casual riding. In time, you may wish to purchase a longer stem with less rise to get closer to the more efficient and powerful 45-degree back angle described in the advice for fitting a mountain bike. Stems with adjustable pivots are available, if you want to experiment with various positions.

4. Toeclips are much less common since the advent of clipless pedal systems. If you do use clips, be sure that when the ball of your foot is properly positioned over the pedal axle, there's about 1/4 inch of space between the toe of your shoe and the end of the clip. This is necessary to prevent pressure on your toes and damage to your shoes. If your foot size is between toe-clip sizes, either use the larger size and have extra room, or select the smaller size and place washers between the clips and the pedals to gain the necessary space.

5. To verify that your saddle is positioned properly, try riding no-hands or with very light pressure on the handlebar. If you slide forward, angle the nose of the saddle upward slightly.

6. Saddle height (the distance from the top of the saddle to the

center of the crank axle) is not an exact science. Use the following two methods to get into the proper range; then take your body's advice during rides and make slight refinements.

- With your bare feet 6 inches apart, hold a tape measure firmly into your crotch and measure to the floor. (Have a friend help so you're exact.) Multiply this number by 0.883. The result is your saddle height.

- Pedal backward, using your heels. Place the saddle just below the point where you must rock your hips to keep your feet in contact with the pedals.

7. Occasionally check and adjust your saddle height if you are still growing or if you ride year-round. The saddle should be lowered in winter in proportion to the thickness of extra clothing you're sitting on, or if cold weather makes your leg muscles less flexible.

8. No stem change should be necessary when you're bolting an aero bar extension onto your handlebar. Most aero bars have adjustable length and elbow pads with variable height. Your forearms should be parallel to the ground or angled slightly up. Elbow width should be equal to or less than shoulder width.

9. After making corrections to your position, minor discomforts may develop before your body adapts to its new riding posture. This is normal, so resist the temptation to keep fiddling. You'll become more comfortable after a few rides, and then you can concentrate on bike-handling skills and fitness, confident that your riding position is practically perfect.

10. Once your bike setup is honed, carefully measure all the dimensions and keep the numbers in your training diary, toolbox, or other safe place. Then if you crash and knock things out of place or need to install new parts, you'll know exactly how to position them. You'll also have a much easier time setting up a loaner bike or even your next new one.

extension to improve aerodynamics and flatten your back, especially if you get into racing.

12. A flat back is the defining mark of a stylish rider. The correct stem and top tube combination is crucial for this, but so is hip flexibility. When riding, concentrate on rotating the top of your hips forward. If you think of trying to touch the top tube with your stomach, it will help stop you from rounding your back.

13. There are various formulas for determining saddle height, but you needn't be a mathematician to know what the correct height looks like. Your knees should be slightly bent at the bottom of the pedal stroke, and your hips shouldn't rock on the saddle (when viewed from behind). Try this quick method, used at the Olympic Training Center: Set the height so there are 5 mm of clearance between your heel and the pedal at the bottom of the stroke. Add a few millimeters if your shoes have very thin soles at the heel compared with the forefoot. Also, raise the saddle 2 or 3 mm if you have long feet in proportion to your height. For those who have knee pain caused by chondromalacia, a saddle on the higher side of the acceptable range can be therapeutic, so gradually raise it until hip rocking begins; then lower it slightly. Make saddle height changes 2 mm at a time, to avoid leg and knee strain.

14. The saddle should be level, which you can check by laying a straightedge along its length. A slight downward tilt may be more comfortable if you're using an extreme forward position with an aerodynamic bar and elbow rests, but too much causes you to slide forward and place excessive weight on your arms.

15. To determine fore/aft saddle position, sit comfortably in the center of the saddle with the crankarms horizontal. Drop a plumb line from the front of your forward kneecap. It should touch the end of the crankarm. This is the neutral position, and you should be able to achieve it by loosening the seatpost clamp and sliding the saddle fore or aft. Climbers, time trialists, and some road racers prefer the line to fall a centimeter or two behind the end of the crankarm to increase leverage in big gears. Conversely, track and criterium racers like a more forward position to improve leg speed. Remember, if your reach to the handlebar is wrong, use stem length to correct it, not fore/aft saddle position.

16. Determining frame size is complicated by the variety of ways in which manufacturers measure their bikes. Most use centimeters, measuring from the center of the bottom bracket axle to the center or top of the top tube. However, the increasing popularity of "compact" frame designs, with their radically sloping top tubes, has created mass confusion. Our advice: Ignore the manufacturer's stated sizing and go with what's comfortable.

17. By sliding rearward or forward on the saddle, you can emphasize different muscle groups. This can be useful on a long climb. Moving forward accentuates the quadriceps muscles, on the fronts of the thighs, whereas moving back emphasizes the opposite side, the hamstrings and glutes.

18. Notice your footprints as you walk from a swimming pool or in sand. Some people are pigeon-toed and others are duck-footed. To prevent knee injury, strive for a cleat position that accommodates your natural foot angle. Make cleat adjustments on rides until you feel right, or pay a shop to do it, using a fitting device. Better still, use a pedal system that allows your feet to pivot freely ("float") several degrees, thus making precise adjustment unnecessary. Position cleats fore/aft so the widest part of each foot is directly above or slightly in front of the pedal axle.

19. The trend is toward longer crankarms. These add power but may inhibit pedaling speed. In general, if your inseam is less than 29 inches, use 165 mm crankarms; 29 to 32 inches, 170 mm; 33 or 34 inches, 172.5 mm; and more than 34 inches, 175 mm. Crankarm length is measured from the center of the fixing bolt to the center of the pedal mounting hole. It's usually stamped on the back of the arm.

Mountain Bike

20. Spontaneous (sometimes unwanted) dismounts are a part of riding off-road. Consequently, you need lots of clearance between you and the top tube for obvious reasons. The ideal mountain bike size is about 4 inches smaller than your road bike size. This isn't as critical if you'll be riding only on pavement or smooth dirt roads, but there's no advantage to having a frame any larger than the smallest size that provides enough saddle height and reach to the handlebar. Smaller frames are lighter, stiffer, and more maneuverable. Because manufacturers specify frame size in different ways, use the stand-over test: When you straddle the bike while wearing your riding shoes, there should be a minimum of 4 inches between your crotch and the top tube.

21. Seatpost lengths of 350 mm are common, so a lot of post can be out of the frame before the maximum extension line shows. For efficient pedaling, your knee should remain slightly bent at the

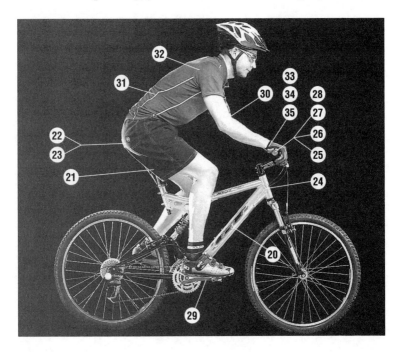

bottom of the pedal stroke. If you switch between mountain and road bikes, take care to maintain the same saddle height; otherwise, you're inviting injury. On steep descents, some riders drop the saddle drastically to keep their weight low and rearward, but others just slide their butts off the back.

22. Most off-road riders prefer a level saddle, but some (including many women) find a slight nose-down tilt avoids pressure and irritation. Others go slightly nose-up, which helps them sit back and lessen strain on their arms. The key word: Experiment.

23. Don't use fore–aft saddle adjustments to change your reach to the handlebar—that's why stems come with different extensions. Use the same procedure described for road bikes, and again, if you're switching between mountain and road, strive for a similar saddle–pedal relationship.

24. Mountain bike stems come in a huge variety of extensions (from 60 to 150 mm) and rises (from −5 to +25 degrees). For good control, the stem should place the bar an inch or two below the top of the saddle. This helps put weight on the front wheel so it's easier to steer on climbs and less likely to leave the ground. The extension should allow comfortably bent arms and a straight back. A longer and lower reach works for fast cruising and steep climbs, but a higher, closer hand position affords more control on difficult trails.

25. An end-to-end handlebar width measurement of 21 to 24 inches is common. Wider bars provide more leverage and therefore control in difficult terrain; narrower bars quicken the steering and allow you to sneak through tight trees. Remember, if the bar is too wide, you can trim it with a hacksaw or a pipe cutter, but if it's too narrow, you're going shopping.

26. Bars can be straight or have up to 11 degrees of rearward bend per side. The choice is strictly one of arm and wrist comfort. Be aware that changing the sweep also changes your reach to the grips and could require a different stem length.

27. If you're having trouble getting comfy, try a "riser bar" with an upward bend. Not only will it increase comfort; it will also provide more control in tricky terrain.

28. Bar ends are great for climbing leverage and achieving a longer, lower position on flat fire roads or pavement. Angle them slightly upward. Models that curve inward help protect your hands and are less likely to snag brush on a tight singletrack. If you're thinking of installing bar ends, make sure your handlebar can accept them; some ultralight bars are simply too fragile.

29. Manufacturers usually vary crankarm length with frame size. For greater leverage on steep climbs, mountain bikes may come with crankarms 5 mm longer than those on a road bike for the same size rider.

30. Even with the tremendous bump-eating capability of modern suspension systems, it's important to maintain slightly bent arms to help buffer against trail irregularities. If you can only reach the bar with straight elbows, get a shorter stem or a riser handlebar.

31. When your reach (top tube/stem length) is correct, you should have a forward lean of about 45 degrees during normal riding, though some modern, long-travel suspension bikes encourage a more upright position.

32. To avoid muscle soreness and fatigue, don't hunch your shoulders. Tilt your head every few minutes to stave off tight neck muscles. Better yet: Stop to admire the scenery.

33. Grasp the bar just firmly enough to maintain control. A relaxed grip will keep you feeling fresher—and therefore more in control.

34. Set the brake levers close to the grips, and angle them so you can extend a finger or two around each and still hold the bar comfortably. With today's powerful braking systems, only one or two fingers are needed to achieve stop-on-a-dime braking power.

35. Your wrists should be straight when you're standing over the saddle and braking, as on a downhill. Always ride with your thumbs wrapped under the bar so your hands can't slip off.

3

109 TIPS FOR SKILL BUILDERS

Almost every adult knows how to ride a bike. But there's a big difference between riding a bike and *riding* a bike. The former will get you from point A to point B; the latter will do it with efficiency, speed, and style. Now, which would you rather do? We thought so. Read on.

1. The quickest way to get better? Ride with people who are a bit faster, stronger, and more skilled than you. You won't get as fit or learn as much if you always ride alone or with people who are at your level or below.

2. Joining a bike club and going on group rides is the best way for a new cyclist to learn firsthand about the sport. Ask at your local bike shop; they likely host rides.

3. Put your left foot down when stopping to prevent greasy chainring "tattoos" on your right calf.

4. To get the most life from a pair of cleats, switch them when the one you usually put on the ground shows signs of wear. Before doing this, outline their position on the soles of your shoes so you can remount them correctly.

5. If climbing isn't your forte, move to Kansas. Barring that, make sure you're at the front of the group when the hill starts; then go up at your pace. If you gradually drift back, you'll still be with everyone (or close behind) at the top.

6. During every ride, work on developing a smooth, round pedal stroke. To eliminate inefficient up-and-down pedaling with dead spots, pull though the bottom of each stroke like you're scraping mud from the bottom of your shoe. Then help the pedal come up and over the top by envisioning your knee trying to touch the handlebar.

WAYS TO KEEP DRIVERS FRIENDLY

1. Keep right. If there's a wide, clean, safe shoulder, use it. One thing that always irritates motorists is a cyclist riding in the traffic lane when a shoulder is present.

2. When riding with a friend, ride side by side only when it won't cause traffic to back up or pass dangerously.

3. Don't force vehicles to repass you needlessly. At a stoplight, stay behind the last car instead of going ahead of drivers who may have just had difficulty passing you safely. Next time, they might not be so careful.

4. Ride predictably. Maintain a straight line. Use hand signals when turning or changing lanes.

5. Stay off busy roads. Drivers will be uptight enough without your being in their way. Find an alternate route out of the main traffic flow.

6. Don't provoke a reaction. Don't circle in front of stopped cars or lean on one while waiting for a light.

7. Be gracious. Motion a driver to make his turn in front of you if you'll be slow getting under way. Who knows? That driver might look a bit more kindly on the next cyclist down the road.

8. Obey all traffic laws. Don't run lights or stop signs, or zip through construction zones. When cyclists disregard the rules of the road, drivers have a right to feel annoyed and even vindictive. To get respect, you need to show respect.

7. On a narrow road with a shoulder that's damaged or missing, take the lane to prevent cars from passing you when it's not safe. Then move over as soon as conditions permit. Remember: You pay taxes, too. It's your road as much as theirs.

8. Communication is the key to safe group rides. When you're at the front, make sure everyone knows of approaching turns, stops, and hazards by calling them out loud and clear.

9. If you don't have a chance to slow for an obstacle such as railroad tracks or a pothole, quickly pull upward on the handlebar to lift your front wheel. You may still damage the rear wheel or it might suffer a pinch flat, but you'll prevent a front-end impact that could cause a crash.

10. To build your confidence in a paceline, start by staying one bike length from the rider in front; then gradually close the gap as your experience and ability increase. Once you can ride comfortably within a wheel's length, you'll be getting most of the benefit of drafting, which can reduce by 35 percent the effort it takes to maintain a given speed.

11. Don't stare at the rear wheel you're following in a paceline. Let your peripheral vision keep tabs while you look a couple of riders ahead to see what they're doing. Then you'll be prepared if something happens to make them veer or change speed. Remember, a paceline is like a Slinky. What happens at the front quickly flows to the back.

12. For safety, don't brake in a paceline. Doing so will slow you too much, open a gap, and possibly cause a dangerous chain reaction. Instead, if you begin to overtake the rider in front, ease your pedal pressure, sit up to catch more wind, or move out to the side a bit. Once you've lost enough speed, tuck back in line and smoothly resume pedaling.

13. Don't overlap someone's rear wheel. If that rider should veer and hit your front wheel even lightly, you're likely to eat pavement.

14. When taking the lead position in a paceline, don't accelerate. Maintain the same speed as when drafting so you don't cause gaps to open between the other riders.

15. If you're leading a paceline up a hill, keep your cadence and pedal pressure constant by shifting to a lower gear. Standing and jamming is dangerous to the riders behind you.

16. When you must stand on a climb, it's easy to decelerate and strike the front wheel of a following rider. Here's how to avoid it: If you favor your right leg, stand up just as it's beginning the downstroke. Don't stand when you can't apply pressure at the same time. Even some good cyclists do this incorrectly, so try to notice who they are. Then when you're behind one and come to a hill, create a safety margin by automatically dropping back half a length or moving to the side.

17. When you start feeling stiff or tired, change your body position. Stand for a minute, or sit if you're climbing out of the saddle. Alter your hand location on the bar. If you're in a group, do this when you're at the back of the paceline.

18. Occasionally take one hand off the bar and shake it. This relaxes your shoulder and elbow and encourages bloodflow to your hand to prevent numbness.

19. Always ride with your elbows bent and your arms and shoulders relaxed. This prevents fatigue caused by muscle tension. It allows your arms to absorb shock instead of transmitting it to your body.

20. Stretching on the bike is key to minimizing fatigue. Coast, put your left foot down, and then lean far to the right to stretch your back and your left leg. Then do the right leg.

21. Know your fitness. In a race, you have to decide whether to let a breakaway go and save your energy for later, or try to join it.

In a long recreational ride, check your fitness before committing to the whole loop, and consider shortcut or bailout options. Don't let your ego get you in trouble.

22. Pace yourself. Most races are won or lost in the last quarter because that's where fatigue takes its toll. The same goes for long training rides and events such as centuries. If you plan to go hard, wait until the last hour of the ride. Then if you overestimate your strength and blow up, you won't have too many miles of suffering left.

23. Don't tune out. Listening to music on headphones can conceal what's happening around you. You can't hear that truck bearing down on you if you're rocking out. For this reason, riding (or driving) with headphones is illegal in many states.

24. If one of the country's 20 or so velodromes is near you, give track riding a try. It's fun, and it will help you develop quicker reflexes. Because track bikes have a single "fixed" gear (no coasting) and no brakes, you need to think ahead and stay focused, especially when riding in a group. Pedaling a fixed gear also cultivates smooth, round leg action.

25. Fast cornering on a wet road isn't a skill that most people are interested in developing. It's safer to slow down instead. To make any wet corner less treacherous, make it as shallow as possible. Set up wide so you enter from a shallow angle, steer straight through the turn, and then exit wide. In effect, this transforms one tight turn into two shallow ones. Be sure traffic is clear before using the whole lane this way.

26. Don't be ashamed to reduce speed for turns, especially on wet roads. The pro peloton is known to ride through corners at walking speed in rainy races.

27. For wet or soft surfaces, run slightly lower tire pressures to increase the size of their contact patch. For example, instead of

UPHILL SKILL

Follow these rules to improve your climbing technique.

1. Relax your shoulders. Keep them back, not hunched, so your chest is open for full, deep breathing. Loose shoulders also keep the upper body free of tension. You'll be supple, able to move smoothly with the pedaling motion.

2. Keep your back flat and your elbows bent. This is true whether you're climbing from the seated or standing position. Like hunched shoulders, a curved back restricts the diaphragm and limits oxygen intake.

3. Grip the handlebar lightly. When sitting, rest your hands on the wide top of the bar. When more steering control is needed, or before standing, move them to the brake lever hoods.

4. Don't use the handlebar drops for climbing unless you're sprinting uphill. A low position runs the risk of restricting chest expansion.

5. Keep your seat. Climbing out of the saddle usually induces a higher heart rate and therefore requires more energy (at the same speed) than staying seated. Stand only when you can't generate enough power in the saddle.

6. When you must stand, move like a cat. First, shift to a higher gear (next-smaller cog) in order to maintain speed when your cadence naturally decreases. Rise smoothly from the saddle without disturbing the bike's forward motion. Doing it right will preserve your rhythm and pace, as well as keeping the rider on your wheel from running into you.

7. On long climbs, stand periodically to stretch your muscles and enhance circulation, even if the steepness of the grade doesn't require it.

using the full recommended pressure of about 110 psi in your road tires, deflate them to 80 or 90 psi. Bleed just enough air so the tires deform slightly under your weight, but not so much that they squash like radial car tires. You don't want them squirming

8. Break long climbs into tolerable chunks. Don't think about how far it is to the peak; instead, concentrate on making it to the next road sign or birch tree.

9. Choose a gear that allows you to "spin" at 80 rpm or more. High cadences reduce the workload on your muscles and allow you to accelerate more quickly to follow a riding partner or competitor.

10. Install a triple front chainring on your road bike. Not so long ago, only mountain bikes came equipped with triple chainrings. These days, it's not uncommon to find them on race-quality road bikes. A triple will allow you to climb longer and more efficiently and just might save your knees.

11. Eat and drink long before the climb so the increased intensity of the ascent doesn't upset your stomach.

12. When the going gets tough, focus on the white line along the road's shoulder, or the wheel in front of you. This will help distract you from the pain of hard climbing.

13. If you start to "blow up," back off just a notch. You'll be amazed at how much better you'll feel going just 5 percent easier. And you'll hardly notice the difference in your speed.

14. When climbing off-road over slippery terrain, concentrate on pedaling smoothly so as not to spin the rear wheel. Keep your upper body low over the top tube to maintain weight on the front end without losing traction.

15. If you want to get out of the saddle on a long climb, shift up one or two cogs before standing. The extra advantage of your body weight will make it easier to turn a given gear.

or allowing pinch flats. This goes for the knobbies on a mountain bike, too. Reduce pressure proportionally—say, from 45 to 35 psi. The new tubeless mountain bike tires can be run at even lower pressures.

28. For road racing, consider increasing tire pressure in the rain. Why? Because then you'll have an advantage of 20 to 30 psi over the traditionalists who bleed air pressure. Your rolling resistance will be down to the minimum while your competitors are squishing along the course on soft rubber. Our advice? Try it only on courses that have few or no sharp turns, and always be careful.

29. The first 10 minutes of a rainstorm are always the most dangerous, particularly if it's been dry for a few days. Oil and dust float to the surface, making the pavement slick. But as rain continues and washes this slippery film away, your traction may become almost as secure as on a dry road. Painted lines and steel surfaces (manhole covers, grates, railroad tracks, bridge decks and expansion joints) are always greasier than the surrounding asphalt.

30. To get safely through a sandy or gravel-strewn turn, straighten the bike until you're past the loose stuff, and then resume turning. Avoid braking or excessively leaning the bike on a loose surface. Shift your weight back to help the bike track straight.

31. If you come into a turn too hot, don't lock up the brakes. Instead, stop pedaling with the inside pedal up, as shown in the photo, so it won't strike the road when you lean the bike. Slide to the rear of the saddle. Put your weight on the outside pedal. Push the bike down and into the turn with your inside arm, away from your body. You can carve a very tight, fast turn this way. Any braking should take place before you start the lean, using the rear brake only.

32. The ability to sprint—whether to escape a snarling dog, cross an intersection ahead of traffic, or win a race—comes with practice. But sprint training can be painfully boring unless you make it into a game. So hone your technique by sprinting for town line signs or other landmarks during club rides or group training. It's an informal, fun way to add speedwork.

33. Don't downshift too soon on a hill. It'll steal your momentum and leave you spinning furiously to no effect.

34. Don't downshift too late on a hill. Instead of wasting energy by pushing a large gear and downshifting only after your legs are spent, keep your cadence up in your comfort zone. If this is around 80 rpm on a climb, stay in your gear until your cadence slows slightly. Then shift lower to restore rpm and avoid bogging down.

35. Learn to do a "trackstand" and you may never again have to dab a foot down at a stoplight. It's easiest when the pavement is sloping uphill. When the slope is from right to left, place your right crankarm at 2 o'clock as you stop, and turn the front wheel into the grade. The front wheel will try to roll backward, but by applying light pressure to the right pedal, you'll counter this force and put the bike into a stalemate position. Voilà! A track-stand. (The name comes from a tactic used by velodrome racers.) Reverse these instructions for a slope from the left. If the road is flat, you'll have to depend more on your balance and brakes. Practice in a driveway, not in real traffic!

36. For long climbs, use a gear you can pedal at about 80 to 90 rpm. This will be a relatively low gear that helps conserve energy for the entire climb. If you have something left as the top comes into view, you can upshift one cog to gain speed. Then anyone who has been struggling in a higher gear will drop right off your wheel. This is one reason Lance Armstrong was so devastating in the mountains of the Tour de France.

37. Whether you should sit or stand on climbs is a matter of personal preference. But generally, stay in the saddle on long, steady hills to conserve energy. On short climbs, you can stand and jam to maintain momentum. Just don't underestimate the climb, or you'll be stuck in a gear you can't turn over.

38. Even though it's more efficient to sit on a long climb, it's good to stand occasionally for a couple dozen pedal strokes. This increases comfort by changing body position and altering the muscles that are bearing the strain.

39. Cross railroad tracks near the side of the road. It's usually smoother there than in the center. Always cross with your wheels perpendicular to the rails. If the tracks are angled, you may have to set up on the extreme left or right of the shoulder and then cut back across. Be extremely careful if the tracks are wet.

40. To smooth a jerky pedal stroke, practice pedaling down a long, gradual hill in a low gear (for example, 39×17 teeth) as fast as possible without bouncing in the saddle. Riding a fixed gear, if you have access to one, can do wonders for smoothing out your stroke.

41. Take a cue from fighters who shadowbox to refine technique. Early or late in the day, watch your shadow as you ride, checking for flaws in position, form, and pedaling style.

42. When climbing, think of pedaling across the stroke, rather than simply up and down. Strive to apply power horizontally through the bottom and top. This involves more leg muscles and enhances momentum.

43. To stave off muscle fatigue during hard, sustained pedaling, learn to "float" each leg every three or four strokes. Simply let your foot fall without exerting force. Legendary French time trial specialist Jacques Anquetil reportedly used this technique.

44. Develop bike-handling skills by riding with others on a grassy field. Play tag, ride the length of the field leaning into one another, pick up sticks without dismounting, and purposely touch wheels to learn how your bike reacts. Falling on soft ground won't hurt at slow speed, except if you land on your head, so always wear your helmet.

45. Most riders find they can't breathe as well if they grip the handlebar drops when climbing. Besides, the aerodynamic advantage of a low position isn't important at climbing speeds. Instead, grip the bar top or the brake lever hoods to sit up and help your diaphragm expand. Wider bars help "open up" your shoulders and increase your breathing efficiency.

46. Anticipate shifts to lower gears (such as when starting a climb) so you can make them before you're applying heavy pedal pressure. Should you misjudge, reduce your leg force for one revolution the instant you make the shift, allowing the chain to move with minimal delay and less grinding.

47. To climb faster, begin in a lower gear than you need and shift up as you ascend.

48. When you're braking in the rain or anytime your rims are wet, remember that the first few wheel revolutions will do nothing but wipe moisture from the rims and pads. Allow yourself more stopping distance. Once squeegeed dry, the brakes may suddenly take hold. Be ready to loosen your grip on the levers as soon as you feel the grab, or you could skid.

49. Normally, applying the front brake harder than the rear is the most effective way to stop. On slick surfaces, however, braking hard up front invites a front-wheel skid, which will almost always cause a crash. Better to emphasize the rear brake. It's much easier to keep things under control if it's the rear wheel that momentarily locks.

50. During an event, remember that a full water bottle weighs about a pound and a half. If you're approaching a long climb with two or three full bottles, drink your fill and dump what you won't need before reaching the next stop or feed zone.

51. When descending, your bike will be stabler if you're pedaling, not just coasting. Always descend in a high gear to retain the ability to accelerate if the situation calls for it.

52. Change your hand position often. On a drop bar, go from the tops of the lever hoods to the hooks, to the drops, and all points between. Each change alters the angle of your back, neck, arms, and wrists, emphasizing certain muscles as others are stressed less. This is a key to comfort on long rides.

53. For a comfortable position that rests the arms by eliminating the need to grip with the hands, ride with the brake lever hoods between your index and middle fingers.

54. Hand positions are limited on mountain bikes and hybrids with flat handlebars. If you do long rides or lots of climbing, install bar ends to give yourself an alternative grip that improves comfort and efficiency.

55. Most flat tires happen when something sharp sticks to the tread and then works through during subsequent revolutions. Keep your eyes and ears alert for telltale signs that a potential puncture producer has been picked up. Stop immediately and remove it. Broken glass is common on the shoulder; keep an eye out for it, and don't ride through it if possible.

56. Wipe your road tires while riding. Even if they have a protective Kevlar belt, it pays to brush the tread every few minutes. Use the palm of your gloves. Be very careful when reaching back to the rear tire until you get the hang of it. A hand jammed between the spinning wheel and seat tube can break a bone in your hand, or send you flying.

57. Don't ride the brakes on a long descent. It heats the rims and could cause a clincher tire to blow off or a tubular tire's glue to melt. Instead, apply the brakes briefly and firmly to control your speed; then coast until you need to slow again. This way, the rims and brake pads will cool between applications.

58. Reduce the need to brake on descents by sitting up to let your body catch the wind. This can take 10 mph off your speed. Standing on the pedals exposes even more of your body to the wind.

59. To stop bike shimmy on descents, accelerate or decelerate from the speed where it occurs. It also helps to lean forward, putting more weight on the front wheel, and to clamp the top tube between your knees. Resting a knee on the top tube during descents can prevent shimmy from occurring.

60. When you enter a turn too fast, it's better to stand hard on your outside pedal and lean the bike way over than to jam on the brakes. Braking will only straighten the bike and send you off line. If leaning causes your wheels to slip and you go down, road rash is a much better fate than sailing across the lane into traffic, a guardrail, or a tree.

61. To sprint better, use these tips from Canada's best-ever pro road racer, Steve Bauer.

- Don't move your upper body too much. Let your back serve as a fulcrum with your bike swaying back and forth beneath it.

- Don't move your weight too far forward. Your shoulders should not go past the front wheel axle. Too much weight on the front wheel makes the bike hard to handle.

- Pull on the bar with a rowing motion to counter the power of your legs. This helps transfer your energy to the pedals rather than into wasted movement.

62. During a headlong crash, the ideal response is to break your fall with outstretched arms but immediately let your elbows collapse. Tuck your chin to your chest and roll across one shoulder and your back. This dissipates the force of the impact and protects your helmeted head (you are wearing a helmet—right?). Make tucking and rolling second nature by practicing on a gym mat or a soft grassy area.

63. If you ride on roads at night, it's safest to use three lights. Aim one to cast a beam on the pavement, far enough ahead to let you ride as fast as you want. Aim the other light higher, at motorists' eye level. This will catch their attention. They may not notice a light pointed at the road. A blinking red light attached to your seatpost makes you visible from behind.

64. Especially on descents, reduce your speed at night to stay within the reaction zone of your headlight beam.

65. When riding on a Friday or Saturday night, avoid main thoroughfares, particularly in the vicinity of bars and nightclubs. Drunk drivers are everywhere on weekend nights. Be extra cautious at intersections.

66. Don't fight to keep your speed in a headwind. Instead, use it as an opportunity to slow down and work on your pedaling form or, if you're riding in a paceline, to trade pulls efficiently. In terms of pedaling effort, a cyclist who travels 18 mph through calm air will have to work about twice as hard to maintain that speed into a 10 mph headwind.

67. Because your body accounts for approximately 70 percent of air resistance, your immediate response when you're turning into the wind should be to become more aerodynamic by hunkering down on the handlebar drops or bar ends. Conversely, take advantage of a tailwind by sitting higher to use your body as a sail.

68. Wind usually increases during the day, so start a morning ride on a route that takes you into the breeze. You could very well have a brisk tailwind pushing you along on your return.

69. Beware of a crosswind from the left. You'll naturally lean into it in order to ride a straight line. Then when traffic passes and momentarily blocks the wind, you may veer left into the lane. Help prevent this by expecting it. Keep your elbows and grip relaxed to enable quick responses to changing wind velocity and direction.

70. If you have difficulty riding a safe, straight line along the road's edge, try these pointers.

- Focus your eyes about 20 feet ahead when riding at 10 to 15 mph, and 1 foot farther for every additional mph. This will provide enough time to make smooth corrections when you see things in your way. Look ahead to where you're going, not down at where you already are.

- Keep your hands, wrists, and elbows relaxed.

- Practice riding without wavering by keeping your wheels on the painted lines of an empty parking lot or a deserted country road. You'll find it much easier if you're looking well ahead rather than in front of your wheel. Once you've got the knack, work on staying straight when you turn your head to look to the side or behind.

- When on busy roads, strive to ride an imaginary rail that is 6 inches to the left of the white road-edge line.

71. Look where you want your wheels to go, not where you're afraid they might go. This is important on roads or trails with drop-offs or other hazards along the edge. A bike has an uncanny way of going right to the spot where its rider looks.

72. The key to making it safely through unexpected patches of sand or gravel is to stay relaxed. Resist the temptation to jam on the brakes, shift your weight back, and give the bike enough freedom to drift in the direction it wants.

73. When approaching a loose or bumpy surface, shift one gear higher (smaller cog) and reduce your cadence. By pedaling slower against more resistance, you create a stable platform for your feet, which gives you more control than if you were spinning or coasting.

74. If forced from the road onto an unpaved shoulder, react instantly by sliding back on the saddle, reducing your cadence, and maintaining a firm yet sensitive grip on the handlebar. Stay on the shoulder until you find a safe and convenient "on ramp" back to the pavement.

75. The safest way to ride no-hands is to shift into a moderate gear and smoothly release the handlebar as you straighten your back and sit upright. Staying hunched forward puts too much weight over the front wheel and causes an erratic path down the road.

76. Nobody likes an attacking dog, but keep your head when you spot one coming at you. If you can't outsprint it, yell "No!" or "Stay!" or "Go home!" Repeated several times in a strong voice, these commands mimic the dog's owner and may put an end to the chase.

77. When a mean dog is running right alongside, you need to buy time until you can ride out of its small but well-defined territory. You can squirt your bottle in its face, raise your tire pump menacingly and swing it if you have to (won't work with a mini-pump), or use a commercial dog repellent. Usually, a stream of water on the muzzle is all it takes.

78. If nothing works to stop a dog and you're cornered, get off your bike. The lack of motion may end the threat. Keep your bike between yourself and the dog until either it wanders off or help arrives.

79. For easier breathing that also contributes to a low riding position and a flat back, try this: Instead of actively drawing air into the lungs and then passively letting it out as in normal breathing, do the opposite. Actively push air out and passively let it in.

80. As your effort becomes harder, increase the force of your breaths rather than the frequency. Avoid panting.

81. To make a panic stop, apply both brakes simultaneously, giving slightly more pressure to the front brake because it's more powerful. Using only the front brake may send you over the handlebar, whereas using only the rear will simply lock up the tire and won't stop you fast enough. To counter the bike's tendency to pivot forward over the front wheel, stay low and extend your arms to push your butt off the back of the saddle.

82. To develop the fast, smooth spin it takes for a good sprint, occasionally pedal your climbing gear on descents instead of shifting up.

83. Here are former Olympic sprint champion Mark Gorski's tips for keeping control during hard accelerations.

- On a road bike, firmly grip the handlebar drops midway between the bend and the end.

- Keep your elbows slightly bent to help you steer a straight line.

- Pull evenly on the handlebar.

- Don't hold your breath, a common mistake during hard efforts.

- Keep your head up.

84. To sprint faster and farther, accelerate out of the saddle for up to 100 yards to reach your maximum rpm; then sit and maintain it.

85. Whenever you make the transition from standing to sitting, gain a few free inches by pushing the bike forward as you drop to the saddle.

86. The trick to jumping the bike over an object or a hole is to begin with a deep crouch. Then sharply spring upward while lifting on the handlebar and pedals to pull the bike in to your body. (Clipless pedals are essential for this.) Keep the front wheel pointed straight ahead so it will stay under you during the landing.

87. To jump over a wide object such as a set of railroad tracks or a cattle guard, keep your speed up and commit to the jump. If you hesitate or back off slightly and then decide to jump, the front wheel may make it across, but the rear won't.

88. When descending through curves, follow an outside-inside-outside line. This technique is based on simple geometry and can be observed in any car or motorcycle race. It reduces the sharpness of the curve and minimizes the lean angle of the bike, making it the fastest yet safest way through. For example, to negotiate a left turn, approach it from the right edge of the road. Drive toward the centerline as the apex approaches (traffic permitting); then exit to the right edge of the road as the corner eases. Conversely, a right turn requires a centerline-apex-centerline course. The principle is the same when riding twisty single-track on your mountain bike.

89. In weather so frosty that even wool socks and neoprene booties don't prevent your toes from getting numb, use an old cyclocross trick: Get off the bike and walk or run for 1 minute during every 20.

90. The next time another rider sails past, move over into his or her slipstream. Without any extra effort, your speed will increase, if only temporarily.

91. Never latch on to a passing rider's wheel without asking permission. It's bad form to just sit there enjoying the draft without offering to take some pulls. The other rider may decline if he's doing a workout, but he'll appreciate your offer and feel less annoyed by your wheelsucking.

92. Sometimes it feels that the wind is always against you. Well, chances are that it is. Only those winds within the trailing 160 degrees of an imaginary circle drawn around a cyclist provide assistance. Wind anywhere in the other 200 degrees works against you.

93. To develop a fast spin, stay in lower-than-usual gears when riding with a tailwind. This boosts your cadence, training you to pedal smoothly at high rpm.

94. When riding a road bike one-handed for any reason, grip the bar on top next to the stem. If your hand is farther out (such as on the brake lever hood), the bike is more likely to veer dangerously should the front wheel hit a rock, bump, or pothole.

95. Ride rough pavement with your hands atop the bar. Lean forward and use your arms to support your upper-body weight to minimize the blows to your butt. Keep your elbows loose to absorb shock. Let the bike shake and rattle beneath you. Keep your thumbs wrapped under the bar rather than resting on top, so a sharp bump won't dislodge your grip.

96. During a climb, choose your gears wisely. If you're out of the saddle and bobbing excessively as you pedal, your gear is too low, causing you to drive the pedals through their power stroke too quickly. Conversely, if you must throw the bike excessively from side to side to accommodate the force needed to turn the pedals, your gear is too high.

97. Use a weight training program to build your climbing power. Squats or leg presses should be the centerpiece. These exercises build power in the quadriceps, calf, and gluteus (buttocks) muscles. For the upper body, rowing exercises develop the strength to pull on the handlebar and balance the force exerted by the legs.

98. During long descents on wet roads, ride your brakes lightly to keep the rims free of excess water and to allow quicker stopping.

99. Never ride your road bike through a puddle if you can avoid it. It's not uncommon to find a gaping hole hidden under the water.

100. To perform a cyclocross (off-road) dismount, shift to the gear you'll need beyond the obstacle. Swing your right leg backward over the bike; then bring it forward between your left leg and the frame. Just before it hits the ground, kick your left foot out of the pedal. Suddenly, you're running.

101. To remount as you're running beside the bike, place both hands on the bar and jump onto the saddle with a fluid motion. Hit the seat with the inside of your right thigh; then slide into your riding position. Find the pedals with your feet without looking down.

102. When riding hard in a big gear, use your arms to help stabilize your hips and butt on the saddle. Push slightly on the bar without using your upper-back or shoulder muscles. Don't pull; it uses energy and is only necessary during sprints and climbs.

103. Keep your elbows in line with your body. When they're bowed, you catch more air and waste energy. In a group, you could bump another rider.

104. On long, gradual climbs, move forward on the seat to put emphasis on the quadriceps muscles on the fronts of your thighs. After pedaling in this position for a while, slide back on the seat to relieve the quads and accentuate the gluteus muscles in your buttocks. These shifts help fend off muscle fatigue and extend your energy.

105. Triathletes and time trialists, you'll need to get used to quicker handling and oversteer (more steering reaction than expected) when you're laid out on an aerodynamic handlebar or a bolt-on aero attachment. This happens because riding in such an extended position puts your hands in front of the handlebar and more weight on the front wheel.

106. If you drop your chain past the inner chainring to the bottom bracket during a shift, don't automatically dismount. Instead, try gently shifting it back on while pedaling. If this doesn't work, you needn't dirty your hands. Turn the bike over so the chain catches on the bottom of the small chainring. Then turn the crank backward to fully engage the chain.

107. Use the whole saddle. Sit in the center for normal pedaling, scoot forward to increase your spin, and slide back to apply more power.

108. Ride like a jockey to extend the life of your road bike's wheels. Sharp impacts cause flats and rim damage, so back off your speed and stand slightly, with bent knees and elbows, to absorb the shocks of riding over railroad tracks, potholes, and other hazards.

109. Stretch on the bike: Your lower back can get sore, especially on long climbs. When the road flattens out, stand on your pedals and pull your pelvis toward the bars to relax your back muscles.

4 ▶▶▶

82 TIPS FOR BETTER TRAINING TECHNIQUES

What's the difference between "riding" and "training"? Good question. Riding is an end unto itself; it assumes no greater purpose. Training, on the other hand, is what happens when you want more from riding. You want to ride faster or farther, or both. Yes, these things will happen by default if all you do is ride, but to get the most out of your cycling, you need to train. Here's how to get started.

1. Start rides into the wind. This way if you run low on energy, you'll be helped by a tailwind on the way home. In cold weather, this tactic will limit the icy windchill after you've worked up a sweat.

2. Don't hit the gas before your engine is warmed up. It may take 20 minutes of easy spinning before you feel ready for real training to begin. To get loose faster, stretch before riding.

3. The best way to recover from a hard effort is to ride easily the next day rather than take the day off. Note that Tour de France riders will put in 1 or 2 hours on the Tour's rest days. Use the opportunity to cycle with family or friends who are normally "too slow."

4. Racers should train by time, not miles, says Greg LeMond, America's three-time Tour de France champion. The reason? "Twenty miles into a headwind is a lot different than 20 miles with a tailwind."

5. Be aware of the mental stresses of training as well as the physical stresses. Says LeMond: "I think your mind will burn out before your body. Your body can adapt to almost anything."

6. Ride on rollers to develop a fluid pedaling style. Unlike resistance trainers, rollers make you balance the bike. They force you to concentrate on a circular stroke no matter what the cadence. The same goes for riding a fixed-gear bike.

7. Whether your off-season pedaling is on rollers or a resistance trainer, make sure indoor workouts are intense enough to raise your heart rate to 70 to 80 percent of its maximum for about 30 minutes each session. Winter provides a psychological rest by reducing your riding time, but don't let your cardiovascular system get out of shape.

8. The key to training with a heart-rate monitor is knowing your heart's maximum beats per minute. You can get a rough estimate by subtracting your age from 220, but it's much better to have it determined by a stress test or a max VO_2 test. Once you have the figure, training becomes a matter of percentages, using these four levels of exertion.

- Less than 65 percent of maximum heart rate to promote recovery
- 75 percent of maximum to build aerobic endurance
- 85 percent of maximum to approach your lactate threshold, the point at which the greatest aerobic improvement occurs
- 95 to 100 percent of maximum, done in short bursts, to train for sprints, attacks, chases, hill jams, and so on

9. Few things in life are guaranteed, but here's one: If you routinely train in the range between 65 and 85 percent of your maximum heart rate, you will become fitter.

10. Cyclists who work full-time or go to school should probably limit their training to 10 to 12 hours per week, according to LeMond. This should be enough to realize your potential, and it protects the time you need for other important things in life.

11. If you're serious about racing, ask your doctor where you can take a max VO_2 test. This is the best predictor of your potential in cycling and other endurance sports. Max VO_2, the measurement of your body's aerobic capacity, is the amount of oxygen you can take in and use during 1 minute of extreme exercise. Heredity plays an important role, as do fitness and physical maturity. Elite bike racers may consume 80 or more milliliters of oxygen per kilogram of body weight (the standard measurement for max VO_2), while average in-shape riders are typically in the 50s.

PLAN YOUR TRAINING YEAR

To reach the podium of the Tour de France, you must pursue cycling as a 24/7/365 passion. That's not feasible (or even desirable) for most of us, but the truth remains: The more you commit to the sport, the more you'll get from it. That's why even good amateur riders approach cycling as a year-round activity. Still, they know that doesn't mean to simply go out and ride every day. Instead, they structure their season to build the components of cycling fitness, one atop the other. Here's how.

- **January/February:** Body preparation. The foundation for your season is established in the dead of winter. This is the time to build overall strength. Alternate cycling outdoors or indoors on a resistance trainer with aerobics, weight training, running, cross-country skiing, swimming, and sports such as basketball. These activities condition and refresh your body.

- **March:** Power and skill. The emphasis shifts to cycling with the use of a cyclocross or mountain bike for off-road work that helps you develop power and bike-handling skills. Continue aerobic-paced road rides, too, when the weather permits. Otherwise, use your indoor trainer.

- **April:** Aerobic base. Temperatures are warming, daylight is increasing, and the new season is near. Continue to build your base of aerobic miles and begin venturing into the hills. The ascents are where you develop the muscle strength that's necessary not only for climbing but for faster riding on the flats.

- **May:** Speed. Time to build a faster top end for the finishing sprint in races or competitive group rides. It comes in handy when the Doberman is out, too. Speedwork sprints, interval training, and spirited group rides are all useful tools.

12. When training by heart rate, don't be concerned about workouts that call for specific gears. Your heart doesn't know what gear you're in. Use what you need to get the intensity you want. Gear selection will change as time goes by because the fitter you are, the higher the gears it takes to achieve high heart rates.

- **June:** Peaking. At the height of the season, you need to know how to have your best performance in certain events, whether they're races or long and fast recreational events. This means converting your solid base of cycling fitness into selected short periods of super performance.

- **July:** Remedial work. By now you have ridden enough to know what you do well and where you need to improve. July is the time to identify your deficiencies in sprinting, climbing, time trialing, endurance, or tactics. There's time to remedy them for the second half of the season.

- **August:** Criterium skills. Many clubs sponsor weekly criteriums during August, and the race calendar is full of these short, fast events. To be successful, you need to improve your tactics, bike handling, top-end speed, and sprints. Doing so will make you a more proficient rider all the time.

- **September/October:** Endurance. As racing winds down, the century season begins. Many cyclists also enjoy long, one-day "epic rides" with friends or alone. This is the time of year to hone the techniques and stamina for these lengthy efforts. The endurance base you build will carry over to the following season if you follow it with a sound winter program.

- **November/December:** Active rest. You've had a great season and are raring to go for the next one. But be careful. Now is the time when the seeds of overtraining and chronic fatigue are sown. Relax from the rigors of the busy summer and fall by playing rather than training. Rejuvenate your mind and body with no-pressure rides and a variety of other sports. Begin light weightlifting to prepare your body for the start of real training after the holidays.

13. If you don't have an electronic heart-rate monitor, count your pulse manually at the carotid artery in your neck. Find it with your fingertip just beside your Adam's apple. Or you can check the radial artery in your wrist at the base of either thumb. Meanwhile, save your spare change. Basic heart-rate monitors have

come down in price over the years and can be had for less than $50.

14. To calculate cadence (pedal revolutions per minute), count the number of times your right foot reaches the bottom of the pedal stroke in 15 seconds, and then multiply by four.

15. Maintain a smooth, fast cadence during training. Road racers spin at 90 rpm or more to maintain flexibility and suppleness. By riding a lot in moderate gears, their ingrained ability to spin helps them turn bigger gears at the same quick cadence, which produces speed.

16. If you're out of shape and just getting started in cycling, begin slowly. Initial rides, whether outside or on an indoor trainer, should be limited to 20 to 30 minutes, 3 days per week. Pedal briskly in moderate gears, but don't get out of breath. As your fitness increases, begin riding 5 days per week for at least 30 minutes, and progress from there.

17. Combine power with smoothness by pulling back on each pedal as it comes through the bottom of the stroke. Imagine you're scraping something off the bottom of your shoe.

18. If you hate headwinds (and who doesn't?), plan routes that avoid them. Use hills, tree lines, valleys, and houses to shield yourself until you turn back toward home and can enjoy a tailwind.

19. If you hate hills, learn to love them. There's not a more natural way to get fit than to ride hills frequently. Have faith that climbs will get easier as they help you develop cardiovascular fitness, muscle strength, and better technique.

20. For safety during late-afternoon training that may extend to dusk, attach a small blinking taillight to your seatpost, and stock your jersey pockets or seat bag with two reflective leg bands and a small headlight.

21. If you train late in the day when the temperature dips, carry a

2-by-2-foot sheet of plastic folded in a pocket. When you begin to chill, stuff the sheet up the front of your jersey to insulate your chest. Do the same for long descents in mountainous regions.

22. On long endurance rides, throw in a couple of 15-second sprints every 30 minutes or so. These relieve saddle pressure, stretch your body, add variety, and develop a bit of speed.

23. Don't be afraid to occasionally push a really big gear. Wait until you're warmed up and conditions are right (tailwind or long downgrade); then go for it. Besides feeling the joy of power and speed, you'll be developing the strength it takes to make good time when the wind turns against you or the road slants upward.

24. During the season, take 5 minutes twice each week after riding to do simple upper-body strength-maintenance exercises such as pullups, pushups, and crunches for the abdominals.

25. To increase fitness and decrease the inevitable boredom of pedaling indoors, play games with your heart-rate monitor. Push to 140 bpm (then recover), 150 (recover), then 160. For a medium-intensity workout, go back and forth between 130 and 150. For higher intensity, strive to reach your lactate threshold or even 5 bpm beyond.

26. When finishing a lower-body weight training program in winter, go directly to intervals and climbing workouts on the bike. Hold off on endurance training until later in the spring. If you immediately follow your leg program with long, slow-paced rides, you'll lose some of the power you gained.

27. If your spouse or riding companion is too slow to ride with you, use a tandem. You can pedal as hard as you like, but you'll never lose your partner.

28. If you have less than an hour to train, you can still get a good workout if you emphasize quality. For example, warm up by spinning easily for 10 minutes. Do five 15-second sprints with

45 seconds between them. Then do 10 intervals of 1 minute hard followed by 1 minute easy. Finish by spinning for 10 minutes to cool down.

29. Getting bored with a training route? Ride it in the opposite direction. You'll be amazed by how different it seems.

30. In sloppy spring weather, ride a mountain bike on pavement. This spares your road bike from excessive wear and corrosion as you build power pushing the heavier bike with its fat tires.

31. To put more fun and variety in winter training, try cyclocross. This is an off-road sport that uses a cyclocross bike, similar to a road bike but with knobby tires, lower gears, cantilever brakes, and a higher bottom bracket. You can also race 'cross on a mountain bike, but any bar ends or extensions must be removed. It's typically done on a hilly obstacle course that requires some dismounting and running with the bike. It's a great cardiovascular workout that develops bike-handling skills, and the lifting and carrying strengthens the upper body.

32. Beginning with your next workout, start keeping a training diary. It doesn't have to be expensive or elaborate; all you need is space to record pertinent data each day. Record both total time and times in your various heart-rate zones (for example, 45 minutes endurance, three 6-minute intervals, two sprints). A diary allows you to objectively analyze and learn from your satisfying progress or frustrating failures.

33. To become an efficient user of stored fat for fuel, go on steady rides of at least 3 hours. Fat needs oxygen to burn, and endurance training puts the oxygen where you need it: in your muscles. The longer you go, the better your body becomes at turning fat into energy. Try for at least two such rides per week.

34. Now a few words for anyone who needs more power for climbing or time trialing (and who doesn't?): squats and leg presses. Either exercise is a great builder of strength in the

quadriceps (the large muscles in the fronts of the thighs) and gluteus maximus (buttocks muscles). These are the primary muscles for pushing the pedals.

35. Lifting weights is good, but bulking up is not. The key to building upper-body muscle strength and endurance for cycling is to perform numerous repetitions with light to moderate weights. This technique produces benefits without adding bulk.

36. Snow is only your enemy if you try to ride through it. Embrace snow as an opportunity to cross train on cross-country skis or snowshoes. Cross-country skiing is an excellent builder of aerobic power and upper-body strength, as well as conditioning most of the leg muscles required by cycling. Skate-skiing in particular is easy to learn, and facilitates training at and above your endurance heart rate.

37. Commute by bike. It's an ideal way to include the benefits of cycling—and more time for training—in your daily routine.

38. Don't train hard more than twice a week. Whether you are doing formal interval training, fast group rides, or club races or tackling big hills, it's all stress on your body. Too much will wear you down. If you separate such efforts with at least 2 days of moderate-gear, high-rpm pedaling that assists recovery, the result should be exactly what you want—greater speed and strength.

39. Take at least 1 rest day each week. A day off refreshes your head as well as your body. Use your normal riding time that day for bike maintenance or for running errands you've been putting off.

40. Be aware of the warning signals of overtraining, a condition of chronic fatigue that can devastate any enthusiastic rider, not just racers. The tip-offs include aching legs, elevated resting heart rate, weight loss, poor sleep patterns, irritable disposition, an I-don't-care attitude, a lingering cold, and general lifelessness. This is often misinterpreted as a lack of form and leads to even harder training. Don't get caught in this downward spiral.

41. Entering the new season, spin for about 6 weeks before you start pushing big gears or climbing steep hills. High-cadence, low-gear riding is what sets the foundation for injury-free training in the big chainring.

42. To develop the ability to sprint and accelerate, do speedwork once a week. This is a training session based on a thorough warmup, then several all-out bursts to top speed. Separate each acceleration with easy pedaling for as long as it takes to feel fully recovered.

43. To improve your maximal oxygen uptake (max VO_2) and develop your ability to sustain fast riding, do intervals once a week. Here's the general formula: Warm up well; then accelerate to a speed that's as fast as you can go for a specified time (anywhere from 30 seconds to 5 minutes or longer). After this "on" interval is complete, back off for a timed "rest" interval that allows only partial recovery. Repeat several times; then ride easily to cool down.

44. For big benefits, do interval training at a heart rate that's within 10 percent of your lactate threshold (LT). LT is the point where breathing becomes labored and your muscles start burning with lactic acid buildup. Determine your LT by riding a 10-mile time trial at your limit. The highest heart rate you can sustain is your lactate threshold.

45. Use intense efforts, such as climbing and interval training, to raise your lactate threshold and, thus, your body's breaking point during exercise. Before you reach your LT, most of your energy is produced aerobically (with oxygen). But after you exceed it, a significant amount is produced anaerobically (without oxygen), and you must soon slow down. The higher your LT, the harder you can ride for extended periods.

46. Even if you ride primarily for fitness, you might like to get closer to your cycling potential. Intervals will help. They improve your

BE YOUR OWN COACH

While some lucky riders can afford to shell out as much as $1,000 each month for the privilege of private, personalized coaching, the rest of us must rely on another kind of personal coach: ourselves. Here are some guidelines to get you started.

1. Set goals. However lofty or modest your aims, you need to identify them and write them down. When your goals are firmly established, every training day has a purpose.

2. Evaluate your basic talent. Do this objectively and honestly. The world would be a dreary place without dreams, but make sure yours are rooted in reality.

3. Evaluate your strengths and weaknesses. A good training plan will maximize your cycling talents and remedy your shortcomings.

4. Ask questions. Get information from experienced cyclists. The most helpful are those who have studied the sport for several years and ride intelligently to maximize less-than-outstanding physical talent.

5. Record your workouts. Keep a training diary so you can duplicate workouts that precede a hot streak. Conversely, when you ride poorly, you'll know what training pattern to avoid.

6. Chart your improvement. Getting better is the name of the game. To be sure your program is working, you need an accurate account of your progress toward greater endurance (century rides) and speed (club time trials).

7. Add spice to your training. Vary your schedule so you aren't doing the same handful of routes at the same intensity all season long. And remember that several days away from the bike once in a while can revitalize your attitude and performance.

ability to keep the pace on club rides and surmount those rolling hills that seem to be everywhere. If you're interested in racing, intervals are essential.

47. If you're a racer, do one interval session and one speedwork session each week. Separate these workouts by at least 48 hours. Assuming your important events occur on weekends, the best days for intense training are Tuesdays and Thursdays.

48. The technique called peaking will help you ride your best in a special event. It requires good all-around cycling fitness, then a 4-week schedule of special preparation. The first 2 weeks should consist of hard training with racing or long rides on the weekends. The goal is to dig deep into your reserves of strength, which causes you to rebound to a higher performance level—if you rest adequately. So, train easily during the 3rd week to recover. Start the final week with hard training during the first 3 days; then taper off to short, easy spinning. After the big event, go easy for a week to fully recuperate.

49. In general, three peaks in one season are the most anyone should try. A physical peak is just one step from a tumble into overtraining.

50. Don't take the day off before a race. If you need rest, do it 2 days before. Take a short ride on the eve of the event, and include a couple of sprints to make sure your bike and body are operating well.

51. To improve endurance, do one long ride each week. The key is to maintain a steady, brisk pace for the distance. If you wear a heart-rate monitor, try to go the whole way at 75 to 80 percent of your maximum heart rate. Make sure your diet contains plenty of high-quality carbohydrates to fuel long efforts, and eat frequently during these rides.

52. To improve power, head for the hills. Once a week, do repeats up a half-mile hill, resting on the way down. Go hard enough to put yourself at or above your lactate threshold during the 15 to 30

seconds before you reach the top. Use a gear you can turn at about 80 rpm. This is hard work, so do this training in place of interval or speedwork sessions, not in addition to them.

53. To improve speed, accelerate as fast as you can for distances of 100 to 300 yards in a moderately high gear. Get off the saddle, charge down the road as you build cadence, and then sit and keep increasing your rpm. Make several such efforts during one workout each week.

54. If you have limited time to train, make every second count. Prepare your bike the evening before, and lay out your riding clothes. Or ride during your lunch hour and snack later when back at your desk. If you emphasize quality by keeping your heart rate high, you'll be amazed at how much improvement you can pack into an hour.

55. Off-season aerobic training, whether indoor cycling or another sport, is very important. Just 2 weeks of inactivity will result in a noticeable loss of strength and flexibility, in addition to some weight gain. And in 8 to 12 weeks, the cardiovascular fitness you developed during the season will be all but erased.

56. Swimming improves flexibility, upper-body strength, and breath control. It also conditions legs and hips without overly stressing tendons and muscles. To get cardiovascular benefits, swim at a heart rate of at least 65 percent of maximum for 20 minutes or longer.

57. Running's benefits transfer to cycling if you run uphill or up stairs. This strengthens your quads and calves, and it's a great cardiovascular conditioner. Two cautions: Walk (don't run) when going down, to reduce the risk of knee injury. Also, begin a running program gradually to avoid undue soreness; then run no more frequently than every other day.

58. Indoor trainers are a good way to maintain a degree of cycling fitness in winter, but you'll do even better if you ride outdoors whenever the weather permits. Real riding helps you develop important skills—cornering, climbing, descending—that you can't practice inside. If you can, ride rollers instead of a stationary trainer.

59. Even if you're primarily a road rider, using a mountain bike is one of the best ways to build riding skills and fitness. A weekly off-road outing helps improve your balance, control, and confidence. You'll get stronger from powering through soft surfaces and up steep climbs.

60. To find your most efficient pedaling cadence, you need a cyclocomputer, a heart-rate monitor, a calm cool day, and a mile-long stretch of flat road. After warming up thoroughly, ride the course several times in different gears while keeping your speed the same. For example, do each trial at 18 mph. Record the maximum heart rate attained and the cadence required to hold your target speed. The trial in which your heart rate is lowest will indicate your ideal cadence. Match the results with another test several days later, reversing the gear sequence to nullify the effect fatigue may have on your heart rate.

61. Experiment with different cadences for different terrains and wind conditions, looking for an rpm that maximizes speed while minimizing muscle fatigue and breathlessness. It may be 75 or 95, and it may change as you become fitter and your pedaling technique improves. As a rule, the higher the cadence, the better.

62. More good reasons to train with a heart-rate monitor: It helps you avoid riding too intensely on recovery days or too easily when you should be pushing your limits. It also helps you avoid ride after ride in the murky middle, where returns aren't great for the time spent.

e a monitor to correlate heart rate with subjective feelings of ess and recovery. After a warmup of several miles, ride up a liar hill and decide which of the following applies to you.

- Legs are tired, and pulse is higher than normal.

- Legs are tired, but pulse is normal or low.

- Legs are fresh, but pulse is higher than normal.

- Legs are fresh, and pulse is normal or low.

In the first case, you're definitely tired. Keep the ride short and easy. The second and third cases indicate incomplete recovery from previous rides, making it wise to moderate this day's pace, distance, and terrain. The fourth case tells you that you're ready for hard training.

64. Tree-trunk thighs do not guarantee an explosive sprint. You also need strong back, shoulder, and chest muscles. Without a balance of upper- and lower-body strength, the legs tend to control the bike, making it difficult to accelerate smoothly.

65. You don't need to do 100-mile rides to train for a century. The following tables show two proven training schedules to use during the 10 weeks leading up to the event. The first schedule, "Goal: To Reach 100 Miles," assumes you've been riding an

GOAL: TO REACH 100 MILES »»»

Week	Mon. Easy	Tues. Pace	Wed. Brisk	Thurs.	Fri. Pace	Sat. Pace	Sun. Pace	Total Weekly Mileage
1	6	10	12	Off	10	30	9	77
2	7	11	13	Off	11	34	10	86
3	8	13	15	Off	13	38	11	98
4	8	14	17	Off	14	42	13	108
5	9	15	19	Off	15	47	14	119
6	11	15	21	Off	15	53	16	131
7	12	15	24	Off	15	59	18	143
8	13	15	25	Off	15	65	20	153
9	15	15	25	Off	15	65	20	155
10	15	15	25	Off	10	5 Easy	100	170

GOAL: PERSONAL-BEST CENTURY ▶▶▶

Week	Mon. Easy	Tues. Pace	Wed. Brisk	Thurs.	Fri. Pace	Sat. Pace	Sun. Pace	Total Weekly Mileage
1	10	12	14	Off	12	40	15	103
2	10	13	15	Off	13	44	17	112
3	10	15	17	Off	15	48	18	123
4	11	16	19	Off	16	53	20	135
5	12	18	20	Off	18	59	22	149
6	13	19	23	Off	19	64	24	162
7	14	20	25	Off	20	71	27	177
8	16	20	27	Off	20	75	29	187
9	17	20	30	Off	20	75	32	194
10	19	20	30	Off	10	5 Easy	100	184

average of 45 to 50 miles per week. It will enable you to complete a 100-mile ride. If you've been averaging more than 75 miles per week, try the second schedule, "Goal: Personal-Best Century." It'll help you achieve a personal-best century performance. In each schedule, "easy" means a leisurely ride, mainly to recover from a previous day's hard workout; "pace" means simulating the speed you want to maintain for the century; "brisk" means a lively tempo that's faster than century pace. If your century is on a Saturday, move back the final week's training 1 day.

66. If you train by heart rate, take the weather into account. For example, when the temperature is around freezing, a person's heart beats about 10 percent slower. Thus, if you maintain your regular training levels when it's cold, you'll be getting a workout that's 10 percent more intense. Looked at another way, you can train at 10 percent below your normal levels and still derive the same benefits.

67. You don't have to be a racer to benefit from a weekly program that includes both speed and distance. In order to firm your legs,

lose weight, and become fitter, use a program that combines the following workouts.

- **Moderate days.** To lose weight, forget about the stopwatch and ride medium distances at a brisk but comfortable pace. This conditions your muscles to use stored fat for fuel, as opposed to the carbohydrate-derived fuel, called glycogen, that's used for more intense efforts.

- **Endurance day.** To improve your stamina, go on one long, steady ride every week. Don't worry about distance; just pedal for at least 3 hours.

- **Fast days.** These are crucial to cardiovascular improvement and muscle tone. Twice a week, try to complete 18 miles in an hour (for example) while maintaining a cadence of 90 rpm. Gradually increase speed as you become fitter.

68. Despite its many benefits, cycling neglects to strengthen several important muscles. Here's a list of those you should exercise to improve your riding performance and overall fitness.

- **Abdominals.** They're crucial for stabilizing your riding position and balancing the lower-back muscles that often become highly developed in cyclists.

- **Neck and trapezius.** These muscles support your head on long rides and protect your spinal cord in a crash.

- **Pectorals and triceps.** Strength in your upper chest and arms helps prevent upper-body fatigue caused by leaning on the handlebar for long periods.

- **Deltoids.** These are large triangular muscles that cover the shoulder joint and protect it in a fall.

- **Latissimi dorsi.** In conjunction with the biceps, the lats in the upper back provide the necessary arm strength to pull on the handlebar in sprints or on steep climbs.

69. Avoid total layoffs. During the first couple of weeks, your fitness will deteriorate remarkably fast. The biomechanical improvements that have occurred in a muscle with training decline in what is called a half-time of 12 days. This means that in only 12 days you'll go halfway from your trained state to the level you'd be at if you had never trained at all. And you'll go another half of that distance between days 12 and 24.

70. When you realize that your normal training schedule will be disturbed for more than a couple of weeks, begin a minimum maintenance program. The key is to train intensely for an hour at least 2 days per week. This will safeguard most of your cardiovascular fitness and muscle strength.

71. For losing weight, stationary cycling has been shown to be as effective as other indoor sports. In fact, the energy expended at comparable heart rates is similar no matter what type of exercise machine or activity.

72. Most experienced riders have found that it isn't necessary to correlate the time of day you train with the time you race. It seems to make no difference to physical performance, though there may be benefits in establishing a routine.

73. The following tips will help you squeeze the most out of your time on an indoor trainer. With good planning, you'll be able to get a good workout in as little as 45 to 60 minutes.

- **Warm up well.** Five minutes is the minimum; make it 15 if you're going to do a strenuous workout. Afterward, spin easily for at least 5 minutes to cool down.

- **Devise a workout strategy.** Don't just plug away at one speed. Vary your effort to work on speed, power, endurance, or the ability to recover faster.

- **Use a heart-rate monitor.** Then you can tell if you're riding intensely enough to improve fitness, not just maintain it.

- **Know when to go easy.** Include easy or rest days in your schedule to allow your body to recover from hard training and grow stronger.

- **Keep cool.** Always ride with a large fan blowing on you to minimize sweating and increase comfort. Have at least one water bottle within reach.

- **Ride to tunes, and not the tube!** Television takes concentration away from the effort, while a hard-driving beat can boost your intensity.

- **Focus on your technique.** Use a mirror to check your position, and concentrate on turning smooth circles with your feet.

- **Play mental tricks.** When doing intervals, for example, don't think about the total number you've planned. Instead, concentrate only on the upcoming one so you continue to go hard.

- **Limit yourself.** Don't start using the indoor trainer too early in the winter, or you'll burn out before real cycling resumes. Ride outside as long as conditions permit; then ski or snowshoe as conditions permit.

- **Go high-tech.** Use a computerized trainer that simulates racing and challenges such as hills and headwinds. Or use DVDs that put you through various workouts or create the illusion of riding outdoors.

74. When you return to road riding after a winter of indoor cycling or cross training for aerobic conditioning, build strength by doing a hill workout each week. After warming up, find a gradual climb that's about 1 mile long. Stay seated and use a gear that allows you to pedal no faster than 60 rpm. Think of it as doing leg presses on your bike. As weeks go by, begin using higher gears that you can still handle at this cadence.

75. One of the best ways to improve is to have a purpose on every ride. If you're cycling with a group, practice your drafting skills by organizing a paceline. On another day, do low-gear sprints to develop your spin, or try hill repeats to improve your climbing. On easy days, work on cornering, no-hands riding, or other skills that won't tax your cardiovascular system.

76. There's no reason to spend hours in the weight room each day during winter training. Six exercises packed into 30 minutes are all you need. Choose an exercise for the quads (squats or leg presses), an upper-body pulling movement (pullups or rows), and a pushing exercise (dips or bench presses). Then add two trunk exercises, such as abdominal crunches and back extensions. Finally, complete each workout with isometric exercises for your neck.

77. Forget toe raises or other exercises to develop your calves. According to experts, during pedaling the calf muscle merely acts as a tight wire to transfer quadriceps power to the foot and pedal. So instead of doing calf exercises, spend the time developing the strength of your quads.

78. Use cross training (participation in sports other than cycling) to improve your riding in several ways.

- Training with weights isolates and overloads certain important muscles, thus developing their strength much better than cycling can.

- Engaging in other sports reduces the risk of overuse injuries inherent in doing just one activity.

- It increases overall fitness by conditioning muscles not normally involved in cycling.

- It reduces the mental staleness and boredom that come from doing the same thing every day. It keeps training fun.

79. A simple way to gauge the equivalence of cycling and running (or any aerobic sport) is to forget distance and go by time and heart rate. For example, an hour of riding at a certain heart rate is equivalent to an hour of running at the same heart rate.

80. If you have a lengthy layoff from training (3 months or so), you can get back to within 90 percent of your top form in about 2 months. A good way is to mix high-quality interval workouts on an indoor trainer (spinning classes are great for this) with longer, less intense road rides for aerobic conditioning.

81. Don't let a forced layoff get you down. Longtime endurance athletes don't exhibit a significant loss of heart function when training is stopped for 3 months. In addition, such layoffs don't decrease the number of small blood vessels in the muscles—a key fitness factor. However, muscular endurance does decline rather rapidly.

82. Use videotape or a digital video camera to evaluate your position and riding style. Enlist a friend or your bike club to share the camera rental fee, and shoot lots of tape on various terrains. Then analyze it to check all the parameters of correct technique.

5 ⟫⟫⟫

55 TIPS FOR BETTER DISTANCE RIDING

To some cyclists, a long-distance ride might cover 10 miles. To others, it might cover 10 countries. Still, the beauty of distance riding is this: Not many of us have the genes, talent, or ambition to be successful racers, but we all have the ability to ride well in long recreational events or tours. Distance is the great equalizer; perhaps that's why group century rides and distance rides for charity are becoming ever more popular (and they're a great place to meet other cyclists). Whatever your endurance goals, here's how to realize them.

1. How long can you ride? Your limit will be about three times the duration of your average training ride.

2. To stay in control of your pace during the early miles of a long ride, plan to do a negative split. This is technique of riding the second half faster than the first.

3. To maximize your endurance during a long ride such as a century, follow these guidelines.

   - Divide the ride into segments, and have a strategy for each. For example, instead of thinking that you have 100 miles to ride (which can be intimidating), think of a century as four 25-milers. Ride each one at a pace you know you can handle.

   - Make sure your bike is properly geared for the course. For advice, ask the ride organizer or someone who has ridden there before.

   - Wear shoes with a stiff sole, shorts with a padded liner, and gloves to prevent raw spots and blisters. Also wear sunglasses to protect your eyes and reduce fatigue from glare. A helmet is mandatory, so choose a lightweight model with good ventilation.

- During the 3 days before the ride, consume carbohydrate-rich meals (pasta, rice, potatoes, bread, cereal, grains, vegetables, fruits) and plenty of liquids.

- During the ride, eat before you feel hungry. Good choices are bananas, dried fruit, dates, cookies, bagels, and commercial energy bars and gels.

- Eat steadily but lightly. Stuff your pockets at rest stops, not your stomach.

- Drink before you're thirsty. Consume at least two bottles of fluids per hour on a warm day.

- Vary your riding position. Move your hands from the drops to the brake lever hoods to the top of the handlebar. Stand for 1 minute in every 20 to relieve saddle pressure.

- Stretch. Do slow neck rolls and shoulder shrugs to ward off upper-body stiffness. Stand, coast, and move your hips forward to stretch your legs and loosen your back.

- Ride with a friend who has a similar pace or time goal. The companionship and conversation will help the miles pass more enjoyably.

- If fatigue sets in, don't dwell on the remaining miles. Instead, concentrate on your form, on pedaling efficiency, and on drinking and eating. Rest if necessary, but don't stay off the bike for more than 10 minutes or your muscles may stiffen.

4. Use a backpack-style hydration system on rides that take you far from water supplies, either into the backcountry on your mountain bike or away from towns on your road bike. These systems hold as much as 100 ounces (3 liters) of water, the equivalent of four water bottles.

COST CUTTERS ON TOUR

While touring by bicycle is one of the least expensive vacations you can take (no gas and, if you ride from your front door, no airfare), that doesn't mean you shouldn't use these tips to make it cheaper still.

1. Research your route so you can avoid pricey tourist areas.

2. Anticipate unique problems and be prepared. For example, if you're allergic to bee stings, pack appropriate medication so you can avoid emergency room expenses. If you're leaving the country, check to make sure your medical insurance will cover you.

3. Recruit several friends to accompany you and share all costs.

4. To avoid an expensive parts failure, have your bike professionally inspected and serviced before you leave.

5. If you'll be staying in motels, make advance reservations to get the cheapest rate.

6. Pack a tent and stay in low-cost campgrounds, rather than in fancy recreational vehicle parks.

7. Check out small-town public facilities that may allow a free overnight stay, such as the grounds of parks, courthouses, fire stations, schools, or churches.

8. Compile the addresses of all your high school classmates, aunts, uncles, or cousins thrice removed. After you let them know you'll be pedaling near their homes, overnight welcomes are sure to follow.

9. When stopping at a restaurant, always ask to see a menu before being seated so you're sure the prices are within your budget.

10. Shop at roadside produce stands and farmers' markets for the most reasonably priced fresh foods.

11. Prepare your own meals, using a pot, kitchen utensils, charcoal, or a backpacking stove.

5. Along with your tire repair kit, pack a multitool that has a variety of Allen wrenches, screwdriver blades, a spoke wrench and a chain tool. A second spare tube can come in handy, too.

6. To save a ride in case of wheel damage, carry a spoke wrench as well as spare spokes sized to fit your wheels. Tape them to a chainstay or put them inside your frame pump.

7. Long-distance riders are smart to carry a chain tool. A broken chain isn't common, but it's almost impossible to fix one without one of these small, light, inexpensive tools. You'll find one built into some multitools. If you run a Shimano chain, make sure you are carrying a couple of replacement link pins.

8. Facing a long day in a hard wind? Stuff cotton in your ears. You'll still be able to hear traffic, but the howl will be gone. Somehow a headwind isn't as bad without the roar.

9. To receive free maps as well as brochures on accommodations, attractions, climate, and history, contact the tourism office of the state you'll be visiting and the chambers of commerce in the towns you'll be riding through.

10. On a group tour, take a car or van and have riders alternate as the "sag wagon" driver. Or have a noncycling friend or family member drive. This allows you to ride unburdened by spare clothes, tools, camping gear, and other equipment.

11. Schedule each day so you'll reach your destination by early afternoon. This provides a buffer against unexpected delays. It also gives you time to remove your panniers and explore the area unencumbered.

12. You don't need an extensive wardrobe, even on an extended tour, if you have clothes that dry quickly after washing.

13. Always pack rain gear. (It's the best way to make sure it won't rain.)

14. Check your packing list; then check it again. Cross off anything that isn't absolutely necessary. Otherwise, it's a good bet that you'll unpack after a trip and discover several "indispensable" items that were never needed. You want to be comfortable, but a large part of that comfort is determined by the amount of weight you carry.

15. Pack heavy items and things you don't use frequently, such as tools, in the bottom of your panniers to keep the center of gravity low.

16. For optimal bike handling with loads of 20 pounds or more, put approximately 60 percent of the cargo in the rear panniers, 35 percent in the front panniers, and 5 percent in a handlebar bag. Balance the load from side to side to ensure a stable ride.

17. Front panniers, which are usually one-third smaller than rear ones, are best mounted on a low rack that centers them with the front axle. The farther away from the axle a front load is carried, the more difficult steering becomes.

18. Put a heavy item that you want to keep accessible, such as a telephoto camera lens, in the top of a low-riding front pannier.

19. Tightly roll your clothes and they'll take up less space than if you fold them. Put them in clear, zip-shut plastic bags to keep them clean, dry, and organized.

20. If you take a cooking kit, use the pot to hold your spices, scouring pads, and other small items. To save space, remove food from bulky packages and put it into plastic bags.

21. Put your most frequently used items in your handlebar bag—for example, your camera, notebook, map, sunscreen, and flat repair kit.

22. Never start a tour with full panniers. If you've stuffed in all of your gear and strained the zippers shut, what happens the first time you buy an item or need to stash a half-eaten bag of cookies? Count on it: You will add to your belongings as the adventure progresses.

23. Reserve one rear pannier for soiled items such as shoes or a ground cloth. Similarly, wet items should be kept away from dry ones.

24. Panniers that provide external mesh side pockets are great for drying bathing suits, towels, and laundry as you roll along.

25. Pack the bulkiest items, such as a sleeping bag and pad, atop the rear rack.

26. Although some panniers may claim to be waterproof, don't take chances. Put everything into sturdy plastic bags with tight closures. Line each pannier with a cheap plastic trash bag for extra water protection.

27. The trick to mounting, dismounting, and walking with a loaded bike is to keep it vertical so its weight stays centered over the wheels. Otherwise, it takes lots of strength to keep it from toppling over.

28. To get good photos on a tour, develop the mental discipline to look for picture possibilities. By keeping your camera ready—atop the contents of your handlebar bag or in a jersey pocket—you greatly improve your chances of capturing special moments.

29. Consider using an inexpensive disposable camera. After taking the pictures, you simply give the entire package to a photo developer. Some models are waterproof, making them ideal for bike touring.

30. Digital cameras are ideal for bicycle touring, due to the added weight, bulk, and complexity of carrying film. If you do use a traditional camera, mail your film to a photo developer back home and arrange for future pickup.

31. Although every ounce added to your pannier adds up to pounds, don't deprive yourself of a few simple luxuries. For example, use stainless steel or titanium pots instead of aluminum, which don't heat as evenly and are harder to clean. Take some spices to add flavor to bland camp food. Pack a small pillow for more comfort at bedtime.

32. Hosteling International–USA (HI-USA) is a national nonprofit organization that provides its members with inexpensive accommodations (often less than $17 per night). At last count, there were 85 facilities around the United States. For information, contact HI-USA National Office, 8401 Colesville Road, Suite 600, Silver Spring, MD 20910, or www.hihostels.org.

33. Going overseas? HI-USA can also supply information about its parent organization, the International Youth Hostel Federation, which operates about 4,000 hostels in more than 60 countries.

34. How well you pace yourself is a major key to successful touring. Depending on mileage and terrain, divide the overall trip and each particular day into segments. Balance long rides with short ones, hilly days with flatter ones.

35. Pacing also refers to riding style. Choose gears that permit a cadence of 75 to 90 rpm no matter what the terrain. Spinning a lower gear conserves energy and reduces muscle and joint strain when you're riding day after day.

36. Perhaps the best source of free lodging is churches. Many have bathrooms, showers, and kitchens, and the hospitality is unequaled. In addition, congregational breakfasts and dinners are usually inexpensive and always filling.

37. When approaching someone for a favor, make sure he or she knows you're a bicycle tourist. Most people are friendlier and less suspicious toward cyclists.

TRANSCONTINENTAL ELEMENTALS ⟫⟫⟫

Of all the essentials for saving time and frustration on a transcontinental bike ride, the following are most important.

1. **Good route.** The two most popular cross-country courses are the TransAmerica Bicycle Trail (4,240 miles) and the Northern Tier Route (4,310 miles). These were developed by the Adventure Cycling Association, which sells detailed maps. (Contact ACA, Box 8308, Missoula, MT 59802, or www.adventurecycling.org). If you decide to plan your own route, choose county and secondary roads as much as possible.

2. **Adequate money.** Loaded touring, where you carry camping and cooking gear, usually costs about $25 per day ($10 for campsites, $15 for food). Light touring, where indoor accommodations are used, generally costs about $50 per day. Budget an additional $10 per day for incidentals. Carry an ATM card or an emergency fund of at least $100 in traveler's checks.

3. **Physical preparedness.** Start specific training at least 1 month before the trip, building up to day tours of 55 to 65 miles. Include at least one multiday dress rehearsal, riding your loaded bike on hilly terrain. Then start the trip with several short, easy days. This provides the chance for necessary adjustments and helps you get into the rhythm of cross-country cycling.

4. **Proper equipment.** Wheels and gearing are the most common sources of trouble on extended tours. Use wide, Kevlar-belted tires and wheels with strong alloy rims, 14-gauge spokes. and high-quality hubs. Choose a 27-speed drivetrain based on a triple crankset and a 9-speed cassette. You must be able to pedal at 75 to 90 rpm no matter what the terrain or wind conditions. The lowest gear should be in the 20- to 30-inch range.

5. **Proper attitude.** Be prepared to accept anything because on the backroads of America, you're likely to find it.

6. **Maps or GPS?** Maps are unwieldy, get torn from your hands in the wind, and fall apart in the rain. GPS units are expensive, and if you lose yours, you can't get a free replacement at the nearest gas station.

38. A cheerful, outgoing personality will make you richer than any laundry list of money-saving tips. Strangers have been known to invite cyclists to family reunions, to picnics, and into their homes. It takes just a little effort to bring out the generosity in people.

39. Weekly training for touring should consist of two or three long rides to build endurance. Make these equal to the typical distance and pace you'll ride during your trip. Also do one or two shorter but harder workouts to improve strength and riding skills. These might include hard charges up hills, sprints, or time trials. One weekend day should be reserved for an extra-long ride to accustom you to extended periods in the saddle.

40. Ride a fully loaded bike on one long training ride each week. This will build strength and familiarize you with the idiosyncrasies of handling the weight.

41. A 50-pound load doesn't allow you to stand and work the bike from side to side when climbing. During training, get used to sitting and spinning your granny gear.

42. A 1:1 low-gear ratio (such as a 28-tooth chainring and 28-tooth cog) is necessary if your route has hills. If you'll be crossing the Rockies, go even lower: 32- and 34-tooth cassettes are widely available.

43. If you are sending your bike ahead, the best disposable shipping box is the kind a new bike comes in. These are usually available at no charge from bike shops, if you ask nicely.

44. Most domestic airlines charge extra if you're flying with a bike. This can be as much as $50 each way. To avoid this unfair penalty, don't use a case that indicates what's inside. If the ticket agent should happen ask, just say "exercise equipment" and you won't be charged. Note that hard-shell bike cases look very much like the portable display booths used at trade shows.

45. To prevent maps from taking up too much space, trim away the unnecessary parts. Then throw away each map when you're done with it.

46. Contrary to popular belief, wind more often comes from the east than the west in the country's heartland. On each coast, however, it more commonly blows west to east. Thus, on a cross-country trip, the direction you ride will determine whether you have tailwind assistance at the beginning and end of the ride, or in the middle.

47. There are two keys to keeping a useful, informative journal during a tour: Be honest and be consistent. Don't be self-conscious in what you write, or you'll miss adding life to factual information. Make it a rule to spend at least 15 minutes each day recording what you've accomplished, seen, heard, and felt.

48. If you don't like to write, keep a microcassette tape recorder in your handlebar bag. Then you can record your ideas and feelings quickly and effortlessly.

49. A first aid kit for touring cyclists should contain a selection of adhesive bandages, several butterfly skin closures, a packet of sterile gauze pads, a couple of nonstick pads, a roll of 3-inch gauze, a roll of 2-inch athletic tape, an alcohol-based hand cleanser, alcohol prep swabs, a small container of petroleum jelly, and a tube of antibiotic ointment. Also useful is a pair of medical scissors (blunt tips). Medications should include a laxative, an antacid, something to fight diarrhea, an antihistamine, a painkiller such as aspirin or ibuprofen, and a snakebite kit.

50. Store personal medication and other small items in plastic vials (available from drugstores). Anything that could leak should go into zip-shut plastic bags. Just to be safe, put everything into a large zip-shut bag. Stow it in the same place every trip.

51. Touring alone, rather than with a group, has several important advantages. Solo, you can pedal at your pace without worrying that you're disrupting someone else's style or schedule. You start, rest, and finish when you want and can change plans and routes as often as you please.

52. If a thunderstorm approaches, start looking for shelter in a vehicle or a substantial building. Once you hear thunder, the storm is within 15 miles. It may be moving as fast as 50 mph.

53. If there is no building or car to get into, take these precautions to reduce your chances of being struck by lightning.

- Avoid metal objects such as wire fences, guardrails, and your bike.

- Avoid lone trees or isolated stands of tall ones.

- Take cover in a ravine or under bushes.

- Don't huddle in a group.

- Squat on the balls of your feet, or kneel with your toes touching the ground. If lightning hits, this reduces the chance of its passing through your heart.

54. Before choosing a map, decide how much detail you need. Some people can ride across the country using only state maps such as those found at gas stations, whereas others need more exact guides indicating traffic patterns, rural roads, and topography. In general, a cycling map should indicate essentials such as food stops and lodging. But to preserve your adventure, you don't want so much detail that you know what's around every bend. Investing in a global positioning satellite unit (GPS) can help you pinpoint your location and eliminate map clutter.

55. Use topographic maps to get an overall picture of the terrain. These maps have contour lines that connect points of the same elevation. When these lines are spaced far apart, it means the landscape is flat or rolling. When they're tightly bunched, it's hilly.

6

50 TIPS FOR BETTER MOUNTAIN BIKING

Some cycling techniques apply equally to road and mountain biking. For instance, whether you're riding on-road or off, you need to turn the pedals to make forward motion. Point is, it's a different world out there among the rocks, roots, and ruts of mountain biking. Here's how to navigate it.

1. Clean your bike frequently. This is the most important rule of maintenance. Dirt acts as a grinding compound when it gets between moving parts.

2. If you're careful, you can clean your bike at a self-serve car wash. But never aim the high-pressure wand directly at the headset, crankset, hubs, or pedals. It'll blast water into the bearings.

3. Invest in a chain cleaner. This plastic unit clamps around a section of chain. A reservoir of solvent and series of brushes clean the links as you pedal the bike by hand. It's so easy and effective that you'll use it a lot. Several companies make chain cleaners, and most shops sell them.

4. Never ride through water so deep that the crankset is completely submerged. The flexing from pedaling will let water through the bearing seals.

5. When riding over terrain that requires frequent portages, carry your gear on your body so the bike is as light as possible. A combination hydration system/backpack is ideal for this.

6. To understand more about the moves it takes to be a better mountain biker, there's nothing like seeing great riders in action. Attend

a race and walk to various sections of the course to watch how top riders handle the challenges. For a similar benefit, watch race and instructional DVDs.

7. Shadowing a better rider is a great way to learn new moves. You see techniques and copy them without thinking, improving your confidence and understanding of what's possible.

8. Momentum is your biggest ally. Being too cautious only makes trail riding more difficult. Beginners tend to slow down for everything that looks threatening, and their lack of momentum results in dabs, falls, and frustration. You need some speed to help your wheels carry though stuff that wants to stop them or change their direction.

9. Try night riding to develop a new set of reflexes and intuitive skills. A trail you've ridden a hundred times becomes a new experience after the sunsets.

10. When you spin out on a climb and have to put a foot down, don't surrender and walk to the top. You'll learn more and get fitter if you collect yourself for a moment and then remount and begin pedaling again.

11. To restart on an uphill, first squeeze the brakes to prevent the bike from rolling back. Put the pedal of your strongest leg into position for a downstroke. Release the brakes as you push off; then stay low to keep the front wheel down. Don't immediately try to clip in with your other foot; just put it on the pedal until you get your momentum going.

12. Ride a road bike in order to become a better mountain biker. The benefits are many and include a break from off-road pounding; the development of a faster, suppler pedal stroke; and the ability to do precise workouts such as intervals. It's a time-saver, too, because you can start rides from your front door. Most top mountain bike pros spend up to 80 percent of their training time on road bikes.

13. Adjust the brake cables so the pads don't hit the rims until you've pulled the levers halfway to the bar. Your grip is stronger in this position than when you're braking with extended fingers, and your hands won't fatigue or cramp as fast. However, don't allow so much slack that the levers actually reach the bar, which diminishes braking power.

14. The key to smooth, reliable, nondamaging gear changes when you're pushing hard is to ease your pedal pressure at the instant you move the shift lever. You need to lighten the load on the chain for about one revolution so it won't balk, crunch, or possibly break. Then hit the gas again.

15. Having trouble keeping your wheels on a tight singletrack? Relax. If your elbows and shoulders are loose, your steering inputs will be fluid. You won't be as likely to oversteer and wobble off course.

16. Locate a challenging practice course. By riding the same trail frequently, you can measure your progress and remind yourself about the parts of your game that still need improvement.

17. Lower your saddle when learning to ride steep descents, drop-offs, or other technical terrain that requires lots of body movement. With the seat out of the way, it's easier to quickly change position. As you get hang of it, inch the saddle back to its proper height.

18. Keep an eye on the condition of your brake pads, and replace them regularly. Pads wear quickly in muddy or sandy conditions and on rides with long descents. Disc brake pads are not as susceptible to mud or sand, but still need changing periodically.

19. Use rubbing alcohol as a lubricant when installing new handlebar grips, if they're stubborn about sliding on. Alcohol evaporates quickly and leaves the grips secure.

20. Opt for a smaller frame as long as it still allows the correct reach to the handlebar. Extra clearance between your crotch and the top tube can't hurt during sudden, unplanned dismounts.

13 TIPS FOR FREERIDING GREATNESS

Freeriding is the term used to describe the latest trend in mountain biking, which involves riding over terrain that not long ago would have been considered laughably impossible. But advances in mountain bike technology, particularly in the form of long-travel suspension bikes that soak up huge jumps, have enabled riders to push the boundaries of what's possible on two wheels. If you're ready to make the leap, read on.

1. Suit up. The potential for injury while freeriding is high; mitigate this by donning arm, knee, and shin protectors. A full face helmet is a good idea, and burly gloves should be considered mandatory.

2. Ditch your clipless pedals in favor of old-school, BMX-style flat pedals, which allow you to put a foot down quickly and provide a large platform for all of your antics.

3. Rather than your normal, stiff-soled cycling shoes, wear soft-soled sneakers, which help you "feel" the bike and won't punish you when it comes time to push up a hill.

4. When you're attempting drops, start small and work your way up. You can even practice your technique on sidewalk curbs.

5. When approaching a drop, lengthen your arms (but don't lock your elbows) and lean your weight back. Don't pull up suddenly on the front end; instead, let the shift in your body weight dictate the bike's position in the air.

6. Keep your elbows and knees bent to help absorb landing forces. No matter how much suspension travel your bike has, your body is still your best shock absorber.

21. Virtually any tire will fit on any rim, no matter what their respective widths. In fact, using fat tires on narrow rims makes the tire profile rounder, increasing rim protection and flotation on soft surfaces.

7. Before attempting a drop, a jump, or a section of tricky terrain you've never ridden before, walk it, taking note of hazards and potential bailout options.

8. Whenever your wheels leave the ground, you should land with the rear wheel first, then the front. This is easier to do if the landing is sloping away from you.

9. On super-steep terrain, use your brakes tenderly. Apply them slowly and steadily. Remember: If your rear wheel locks up, you can probably ride out of it, but if your front wheel locks up, you're going down.

10. Beware the wet. Rain and mud are all part of the fun, but never push your limits when terrain surfaces are slippery from inclement weather.

11. Set your brake levers so you can squeeze them with one finger while keeping your remaining digits on the handlebar. Modern disc brakes are so powerful that a single finger is all you need to achieve massive stopping power, and it's important to keep as much of your hand on the grip as possible in tricky terrain.

12. Carry plenty of tools and spare equipment. Freeriding is incredibly hard on gear; expect to get plenty of flats and other breakdowns.

13. Know when to back off. The repercussions of crashing off an 8-foot rock drop are far greater than if your wheels were on the ground. The drop isn't going anywhere; if you're not comfortable, come back and try it another day.

22. To get better traction, follow these fundamentals.

- **Prepare your air.** Adjust tire pressure in accordance with your weight, riding style, surface conditions, and tire size. In most

cases, it should range between 25 and 40 psi. Tubeless tires can be run at lower pressures without risk of pinch flats.

- **Stand up.** This enables you to use the strength of your upper body to dynamically pulse the rear wheel. Do this by bending your elbows, bending your torso toward the stem, and pulling back and up on the handlebar at the beginning of each pedal stroke.

- **Read the surface.** Frequently glance farther down the trail to spot ruts, rocks, downed limbs, and the like. Adjusting your line in time eliminates the need for abrupt changes that jeopardize traction.

- **Maintain your momentum.** Shift to the proper gear ahead of time and hit each tricky section with as much speed as is reasonable and controllable. To handle soft stuff, pedal smoothly and keep your weight back, lightening the front wheel to reduce the risk of plowing in, as shown in the photo above.

23. Watch for changes in ground color. In dry climates, for instance, darker soil usually harbors more moisture and better traction.

24. Improve your climbing ability with these tips from champion off-road racer John Tomac.

- **Shift your weight to maintain traction.** If the rear tire starts to slip on a climb, remain seated and slide back on the saddle. Conversely, if the slope is so steep that the front wheel lifts off the ground, lean forward and slide toward the nose of the saddle.

- **Pick a line.** Look at least 10 yards up the trail so you can smoothly snake around potential momentum stoppers such as rocks, ruts, and logs.

- **Anticipate downshifts.** If you shift to a lower gear just before you're forced to, you won't bog down and lose momentum. This is especially important up front because shifts to smaller chainrings are difficult—or impossible—when heavy pedal pressure is being applied.

25. When you're riding a trail that traverses a steep hillside and something makes you lose balance or stop, always put down the

foot that's on the uphill side, and lean to that side. If you pull the other foot, as the illustration shows, you're in for a long tumble.

26. Trying to decide between flat bars and risers? Flat bars will give you a more aerodynamic position for racing; a riser bar will be more comfortable and provide a stabler platform for steep descents.

27. To find the best brake lever position, first loosen the levers enough so they can be moved. Then get on the bike and assume a standing, crouched position as if you were descending a long hill. This is the situation in which the most braking takes place, so your wrists should be straight to maximize comfort and power and to reduce fatigue. Rotate the levers as necessary; then tighten them firmly.

28. Brake lever tips shouldn't extend beyond the end of the handlebar because they'll be damaged if the bike falls over.

29. Don't brake too much on technical descents. Obviously, you don't want to go too fast and lose control, but you need momentum to get over logs, rocks, and other obstacles. Plus, the faster a wheel is spinning, the greater its resistance to tipping over.

30. When applying the brakes, use them both, but emphasize the front, especially on descents. The front brake becomes more powerful as body weight shifts forward.

31. Lighten up on the rear brake if the rear wheel begins to skid. A turning wheel gives you more control than a skidding wheel.

32. Use these tips when coming to a boggy mess of mud.

   • **Shift to a lower gear (lowest if it looks really deep).** Then slide back on the saddle so you won't pitch forward when the bike decelerates.

- **Keep your momentum.** Stay in the saddle, and pedal with even strokes to maintain balance and forward progress. Use the straightest line because turning in soft stuff scrubs off speed.

- **Go through standing water rather than around it.** Standing water usually indicates firmer, less permeable soil.

- **Apply power.** If you're light, perhaps your tires won't sink and you can "float" through by keeping your pedal strokes smooth and even. But if you're heavy, you'll sink to the bottom and have to power and churn.

- **Ride through downhill mud holes in the middle chainring.** If you're relaxed and smooth, you may carry enough momentum to pedal through easily.

33. Be responsible when riding in muddy conditions. Stay on the trail to prevent scarring soft virgin ground. Ride through puddles instead of around them, which widens the trail. Don't ride muddy slopes that end in streams or ponds. Your tracks will become sluiceways that create erosion. In fact, it's best to avoid muddy trails altogether until they've had a chance to dry out and firm up.

34. Use a thick chain lube when riding in wet conditions. Light lubes are quickly washed away, causing squeaking and excessive wear.

35. Before a sloppy ride, spray the entire drivetrain with a nonstick vegetable cooking product such as Pam. Less gunk will stick, and cleanup will be easier.

36. Chainsuck can occur during shifts to the small chainring. The chain sticks and is pulled up, becoming wedged against the chainring and chainstay. To prevent it, keep the chain clean and lubricated, and replace it and the chainring before they become excessively worn. Avoid shifts to the small ring when you're applying heavy pedal pressure. Running as short a chain as possible also helps.

37. When you experience the misery of chainsuck, it feels as if a stick has been jammed through the chainrings. Stop applying leg force immediately. Quickly pedal backward to free the chain, or get off and turn the crank by hand. Any forward force only increases the risk of damage to the chain, chainring, and chainstay.

38. Perform these three wheel checks once a week to make sure a problem doesn't leave you stranded on the trail.

   • **Overinflate your tires by 10 psi.** If braking has worn the rims close to the point of sidewall failure, you may be able to see cracks under this pressure. If you do, it's time to replace the rim. Be sure to return the tires to proper inflation for riding. This is unnecessary on bikes with disc brakes.

   • **Check each rim's spoke holes.** Bulges or cracks are warnings that spoke nipples are beginning to pull through. In this case, it's necessary to replace the rim.

   • **Wiggle each spoke.** Tighten any loose ones with a spoke wrench until they're as snug as their same-side neighbors. This should put the wheel into true.

39. Check your valve stems regularly to make sure they're still perpendicular to the rim, especially when running low tire pressure. A tube can spin inside the tire and tear the valve. If a valve stem is angled, deflate the tube and realign it.

40. Early in the season, carry a foldable pruning saw in your fanny pack. It takes just moments to stop and cut back limbs. You'll have a better trail that you can enjoy throughout the summer.

41. Severe lateral force from an impact or from sliding through a turn can cause a wheel to assume the shape of a potato chip. To straighten it enough to ride back home, follow these steps.

- Remove the wheel. Position it so the sections that curve inward are at the top and bottom. Hold the sections that curve outward in each hand.

- Place the top of the wheel against a solid, unmovable object (such as a boulder or tree). Rest the bottom on the ground and brace it with your foot.

- Lean forward and push the sides with both hands to bend the wheel back into shape. Spin it to check; then push some more. Keep working at it.

- Reinstall the wheel and see how straight it spins. If necessary, use your spoke wrench to true it between the brake pads. Shoot for clearance, not perfection.

42. Even though a rear wheel's freehub needs minimal maintenance and has no oil ports or grease fittings, repack the axle bearings annually (more often if you ride in cruddy conditions). Some of the grease will find its way into the freehub bearings.

43. Check hubs weekly or after your bike dries following a wet ride. Remove each wheel and turn the axle with your thumb and fore-finger. The action should be smooth, not gritty. You should feel a slight drag as the bearings roll through the grease. If the action is crunchy or the axle spins too freely, it's time for cleaning and repacking.

44. Just because your bike may have sealed hubs doesn't mean dirt and water can't get into the bearings. Cleaning and lubrication proce-dures vary by type. Some hubs have a rubber seal that you can care-fully lift off with an X-Acto knife, exposing the bearings. Others have bearings in press-in cartridges that can be replaced when they become contaminated or dry. Still others have grease fittings that allow fresh lube to be injected, driving out the dirty stuff.

45. Lighten your bike and improve comfort by installing a high-tech handlebar made of lightweight steel, aluminum, titanium, or carbon fiber. Just as light-gauge frame tubes ride smoother than stouter ones, a thin-wall handlebar transmits less shock to your hands, arms, and shoulders. Ultralight bars are less durable, however, so they should be replaced every couple of seasons, or more frequently if you race or crash a lot.

46. Trail access is a privilege, not a right. Do your part to keep trails open to cyclists by always obeying the International Mountain Bicycling Association's rules of the trail.

- Ride on open trails only.

- Leave no trace.

- Control your bicycle.

- Always yield the trail to pedestrians and equestrians.

- Never scare animals.

- Plan ahead.

47. To loft the front wheel over a bump or a low object, simultaneously lower your torso, apply a hard pedal stroke, and lift with your arms. If you shift your weight forward a bit as you roll through, the rear wheel will be free to bounce over lightly.

48. The rougher the trail, the more important it is to relax your body and let your bike do its own thing. Think of your flexed arms and legs as a highly sophisticated and efficient independent suspension system. Crouch slightly off the saddle to let your body float above the bucking bike.

49. The farther you ride into the backcountry (and away from civilization), the greater your need to ride responsibly. It's not only a question of personal safety. If you get hurt in the outback, others will also risk their safety to rescue you.

50. Never quit trying. To progress as a mountain biker, you must attempt to ride everything. Think of it as the Wile E. Coyote technique for cycling excellence. After an unsuccessful attempt, get up, dust yourself off, think about what just happened, and then turn around and try it again. If you still don't succeed, leave it for another day. The trail will always be there waiting for you—just like the Road Runner. You see, that bird isn't defeating the coyote; he's only helping him reach for a higher level of creativity. That's how to look at those nasty trail sections that always give you fits. They're there to help you improve.

19 TIPS FOR BETTER BICYCLE RACING

While it's true that competition isn't for everyone, it's also true that racing delivers cycling experiences you can't get any other way. And it's not as if you have to toe the start line of the Tour de France to get them: Most local clubs and shops promote fun, low-key events that welcome competition from neophytes. Even if you're not interested in organized races, the following tips can help you come out on top of your next group ride. And sometimes that's the sweetest victory of all.

1. Time trials (TT) are a great way to try organized racing because they're safe—it's just you and your bike against the clock. No pack dynamics or dicey wheel-to-wheel dueling. Here are five TT tips from former Olympic champion Connie Carpenter Phinney.

- Avoid mechanical surprises by double-checking everything. Train on new equipment before you race on it.

MISTAKES TO AVOID

Every cyclist makes mistakes; that's how they learn. But there's something to be said for learning from the mistakes of others. Here are some of the most common cycling blunders and how to avoid them.

1. Trying to be what you're not. Learn which events to emphasize and which to avoid. It's generally true that smaller riders climb better, and bigger riders time-trial better. Key factors are body type, temperament, and training time.

2. Not setting goals. Establish daily, weekly, monthly, and season-long objectives. You'll train better if the events are important to you.

3. Going it alone. The most important thing a new racer can do is find knowledgeable riders, train with them, and ask lots of questions.

4. Being impatient. Approach your competitive career as a long-term commitment, realizing that it may take 5 or more years to get your best results.

5. Training too hard. Training hard is the only way to improve, but it's important to rest well, too. Every week, do at least two recovery rides during which your heart rate doesn't go above 120 beats per minute.

6. Overemphasizing equipment. Have a decent bike with a good drivetrain and reliable wheels, but remember that you're competing against other riders, not other bicycles.

- Don't be discouraged if you lack the latest technology. Good position and concentration count for a lot. Lower your stem an inch to encourage a streamlined position. Keep your hands on the drops, your elbows close to your body, your head down, and your eyes up.

- Discipline yourself to ride at a cadence of at least 90 rpm. Good form and a brisk cadence are the keys to speed.

7. Failing to learn from strengths and weaknesses. Train to improve your weak points, and race to use your strong ones.

8. Not having a race strategy. Don't adopt a wait-and-see attitude, letting other riders dictate the action. Devise a game plan that reflects your talents; then refine the plan as the race unfolds, but never abandon it.

9. Using too big a gear for hilly courses. Don't trust the advice of others because strength and climbing styles differ. Try to ride or drive the course beforehand. It's better to install a gear lower than you need than not to have a gear low enough.

10. Being unprepared for wet weather. Train in the rain occasionally because you'll surely get the chance to race in it. You must know what to expect.

11. Quitting. Many new riders don't realize how hard racing is, but dropping out should never be an option. The more you suffer during a race, the greater your chances of doing well. Bicycle racing *is* suffering—there's no getting around it.

12. Not listening to your body. In your eagerness to improve, it's easy to ignore nagging aches and pains, or fatigue. If your body is telling you to back off, listen.

13. Not thinking long-term. If you want to be in cycling for life, you need to think of it as a lifelong pursuit. Don't get hung up on today's failures *or* successes.

- To get good results, you must do specific workouts. Twice a week, ride slightly above your desired time trial speed for a given distance or time.

- Keep a positive attitude. Time trials hurt when you ride them right, and they give you lots of time to think about it. Be assured that it's the same for everyone. The successful riders are those who concentrate on the things that make them faster.

2. Before a race—particularly a time trial, where every second counts—crumple your paper number to make it more flexible; then attach it low on the back of your jersey with extra pins. This keeps it from billowing like a small drogue chute while you ride.

3. To add at least 1 mph to your top speed in a time trial, install an aero handlebar.

4. For information about amateur road, track, or cyclocross competition, contact the United States Cycling Federation, at www.usacycling.org, or by mail at One Olympic Plaza, Colorado Springs, CO 80909. The USCF can send you a license applica-

9 CLUES FOR CRITERIUM RACERS

With its high-speed corners and rocket-fast laps, criterium or "crit" racing is one of the most exciting things you can do on a bicycle. And because it's immensely popular in the United States, it provides one of the easiest ways to dip your cleats in the bike racing waters. Here's how to get your feet wet.

1. Warm up thoroughly and get a starting position in the first three rows. Do whatever it takes to stay near the front when the gun sounds.

2. Be prepared to ride hard from the start. In most criteriums, the initial laps are blazing. Have confidence that the pace will become more tolerable.

3. Fight to maintain a good position in the pack. It's easier (and safer) to stay at the front than to ride at the back and try to move up.

4. Know how to corner safely. Stay relaxed with your elbows flexed so when someone bumps you, you won't lose control. Get confident by riding the corners fast during the warmup. In the race, instead of focusing on the rider in front of you, look at least four or five riders ahead so you can spot danger in time to react.

5. Be a savvy racer. It's after the halfway point that the racing really begins. Because early attacks and breakaways rarely

tion and the name of its representative and member clubs in your locale.

5. For a license to race in mountain bike competition (including a special 1-day license for first timers), contact the National Off-Road Bicycle Association at the address in number 4. NORBA events include cross-country, downhill, dual slalom, observed trials, and mountain cross.

6. The parent organization of the USCF and NORBA is USA Cycling. Check its Web site at www.usacycling.org for up-to-date information about bicycle racing.

succeed, be careful about using your energy to join them. Also, try to notice which riders have poor bike-handling skills or bikes with mechanical problems, such as worn tires or skipping drivetrains, and stay away from them.

6. Always finish strong. Often there's an attack with a kilometer to go and a counterattack 500 meters from the line, and the sprint starts with 250 meters left. You must always be ready to jump. If you aren't a strong sprinter, don't wait for the line to come into sight. Try a solo breakaway; then time-trial for all you're worth. If you can get a gap, you might just make it stick.

7. Don't get discouraged. Because of factors such as drafting, luck, and position in the pack at crucial moments, the strongest rider doesn't always win. In fact, most criterium racers serve a lengthy apprenticeship before doing well. You should never let poor early performances get you down.

8. Don't quit. At some point in nearly every race, you're going to want out. No matter how much it hurts, try to fight through the bad times. If every race is a painful struggle, however, examine your training methods.

9. Develop all of your abilities. Experiment with different tactics because that's the way you'll improve. It's a truism in racing that in order to win, you have to risk losing.

16 TIPS FROM FORMER WORLD CHAMPION NED OVEREND

To do your best in mountain biking's most popular event, the cross country, heed these 16 tips from former world champion Ned Overend.

1. Taper before an important race. Decrease the duration of training sessions during the week in order to build a reserve of energy, but still include some short, hard efforts to keep your body ready for racing intensity.

2. Load carbo and fluids. Emphasize high-energy carbohydrate foods in the 3 days before the race. Also drink plenty of fluids to counter the risk of dehydration, especially when competing in hot, humid conditions.

3. Inspect the course. Ride it at least twice, if possible, and think about passing lanes, places you'll need to shift to the small chain-ring, smooth spots for braking traction, easy sections where you can drink, and the best lines for maximizing momentum.

4. Warm up for at least 30 minutes. A cross-country race is like a time trial that begins with a field sprint. Although you eventually need to pace yourself for the distance and terrain, you must be ready to start fast so you can get ahead of the inevitable bottleneck where singletrack begins.

5. Start smart. Line up near the front, but also toward the side. You'll be less likely to get caught in crashes. Go hard to estab-

7. Avoid following a rider who has damage to his jersey, shorts, or skin. These telltale signs mean he has crashed. Neither he nor his bike may be in the best shape.

8. Always wear a thin synthetic T-shirt under your racing jersey. The garments will slide against each other during an accident, helping protect your skin from crash rash.

lish a good position. Be aggressive about holding it; then settle into your rhythm as the pack spreads out.

6. Pace yourself. As the race wears on, keep shifting to stay in gears that let you pedal efficiently. It's better to use gears that are a little lower rather than too high, at least until you reach the point where you can go for broke to the finish.

7. Use the terrain to your advantage. It's more energy efficient to make time on gradual climbs, descents, and flats rather than on steep climbs. If you want to catch or leave another racer, it takes a lot more energy to increase speed on a hard climb than on milder parts of the course.

8. Rest where you can. To race well, you need to find certain places on the course where you can recover slightly. One tactic is to ease into hard hills before spinning up them. You never want to be at your limit when you start a climb.

9. Know when to dismount. If there's a hard climb that you can't ride more than half the time in practice, it will probably be faster to dismount in the race and run up. Save time by jumping off before it gets too steep, rather than waiting until you're at a standstill and all momentum is gone. Similarly, dismount for drop-offs that you're uncomfortable riding. Better to be safe than risk a race-ending crash.

10. Stay in the saddle as much as possible. Early in the race, you'll be tempted to stand and blast out of turns, over short rollers,

(continued)

9. When you need to gain an extra mile per hour during a sprint, tell yourself to pedal faster, not harder. The latter tends to tense muscles and increase mental strain.

10. "A lot of people forget about mental preparation," cautions veteran racer Ian Jackson. "They think it's all training, and they just go out and pound away. But I feel that 50 percent of success

16 TIPS continued

and across the top of climbs. Sometimes this is the right thing to do, but don't stand unnecessarily. Standing always uses more energy than sitting.

11. Attack to open a gap. Combine your talents with the terrain to get away from other riders. For example, if you're a good climber, do what it takes be first onto the hill. If descending is your forte, get to the downhill first.

12. Be ready to pass. Singletrack is often lined with no-passing zones—things you can't ride on, like rocks, trees, streams, hillsides, and ravines—so you need to watch for wider sections and make the most of them.

13. Stay fueled. For a 1-hour race, two bottles of sports drink are all you need. For longer events, also eat one packet of carbo gel every 40 minutes or so, beginning 30 minutes after the start. It makes no sense to attempt to eat solid food during a cross-country race. Besides the difficulty, it takes too long to digest and release calories.

comes from mental preparation and the knowledge of what goes on within a race. You may not be one of the strongest riders or one of the quickest, but race smartness can help you a great deal."

11. You must know where to light your afterburners in order to reach the finish line at top speed. Before a race, pedal back from the line in your sprinting gear and count pedal revolutions. After about 40 strokes, top speed starts to deteriorate, so when you reach this number, note a landmark. This is the place to begin your finishing sprint. Then you'll be certain that if any riders get past you, it's for only one reason: They're faster. If you wait longer to start your sprint, you won't reach and sustain top speed. If you start sooner, you'll be cooked before the line.

14. Finish fast. Most cross-country courses tend to have a short finishing shoot just past a sharp corner. If you're with other riders, you need to be the first one to the corner so you can take the fastest line through it. Even if you don't have a super sprint, there probably won't be enough distance left for anyone to pass you.

15. Cool down. You can do a lot to alleviate postrace soreness and stiffness by staying in the saddle for 15 minutes after the finish. Stop at your car, wipe off, grab a bottle of carbo/protein drink to start the refueling process, and then take a spin on a flat, smooth road or even around a large parking lot.

16. Evaluate your performance. Race results aren't always what you'd like. If you can identify the cause of a bad performance, be sure to work on the problem until you conquer it. The wrong approach is to accept your shortcomings. Recognize your limitations, but don't accept them. Fix them.

12. To improve your racing performance, use a heart-rate monitor. By knowing your exact pulse during an event, you can maintain maximum energy output and eliminate lapses in concentration.

13. If you want to take a day off, do it 2 days before the race. On the day before, do a short ride that includes a couple of surges to fast speed. This opens your lungs and reminds your body of what it feels like to go hard.

14. Think of a time trial, a breakaway, or other solo effort as the interplay between two absolutes and one variable. The absolutes are your most efficient heart rate and a cadence of about 90 rpm. The variable is gearing. Choose a gear ratio that enables you to maintain optimal heart rate and cadence.

15. Pay strict attention to your form in a time trial. Even small changes in body position profoundly affect air drag by increasing frontal area. These include such movements as turning your head to the side, sitting up, or reaching down for a water bottle.

16. "Don't work on your bike the day before the event," advises former U.S. pro champ Thomas Prehn. By then it should be completely tuned and road-tested. "I've seen guys do a big overhaul the night before an event, then forget to tighten something when they put it back together. During the race, it starts to fall off." Use the eve of a race to relax, knowing that your bike is tested and ready to go.

17. Don't drive a long way to a race without allowing adequate time for a warmup. Legs become stiff when confined to a car for hours.

18. For a concentrated learning experience, attend a training camp. You can learn more with a good coach in 1 week than you can in a year of racing. Camps are available for road riders or mountain bikers. Some are for women only.

19. If you want to be part of a race, stay in the front third of the pack. Any farther back and you lose the ability to help control the race, and become just so much pack fill.

79 TIPS FOR BETTER HEALTH AND FITNESS

Fact is, cycling is one of the best things you can do for your short- and long-term health and fitness. It tunes the cardiovascular system, sheds extra pounds, and, because it's non-weight-bearing, is easy on the joints. But that doesn't mean you get a free pass from all health-related matters. Here are a bucket-load of tips designed to keep you running at peak capacity.

1. At the first sign of foot discomfort on a long ride, slightly loosen your shoelaces and/or hook-and-loop straps, especially at the front of the foot. Feet tend to swell as the miles go by. It's the resulting tightness and restricted circulation that cause pain and the sensation of heat. (Loosen toe straps, too, if you're using them.)

2. If you have back discomfort when you're low on the drops of your road bike, replace the stem with one that has more rise until the handlebar is just an inch below the top of the saddle.

3. If your triceps muscles become fatigued and sore, it probably means your stem is too long. Conversely, if it's too short, your shoulder muscles will let you know.

4. To prevent a sore neck, don't keep your head in a fixed, straight-ahead position. Cock it slightly to one side for a while, then to the other. You'll find it takes less effort to hold your head this way, especially when you're riding in a low position.

5. Wear sunglasses to feel fresher on long rides. Squinting into the sun and wind taxes the muscles of your eyes and face, contributing significantly to fatigue.

6. When you need to take a pain reliever, decide whether swelling also needs to be treated. If so, try aspirin, ibuprofen, or naproxen, all of which reduce inflammation. Acetaminophen fights pain but not swelling.

7. If you drink alcohol, limit yourself to no more than two beverages per day, the equivalent of 24 ounces of beer, 12 ounces of wine, or 2 ounces of hard liquor. Research shows that one healthful effect of regular exercise, namely lower blood pressure, is nullified for those who drink larger quantities.

8. Massage your legs. Pro racers receive a daily rub to promote muscle recovery. If you don't have a masseur, massage yourself. Lie on a bed with a pillow under your head and your legs elevated against the wall. For each leg, reach up to stroke and knead the calf first, and then move to the knee and thigh, always stroking toward the heart to put blood back into circulation.

9. Cycling does many good things for your body, but it doesn't improve range of motion or flexibility. That's why you need to stretch. Work on your legs, lower back, shoulders, and arms. In addition to increasing on-bike comfort, stretching can reduce muscle and joint injuries from overuse or from crashing.

10. Proper stretching technique is to push to the point where you feel the stretch, then back off slightly. Everything should be relaxed. If you stretch to the point of pain, your body thinks it's going to be injured, so it tries to contract against the force. You end up with the opposite response of what you want.

11. To easily fit a few minutes of stretching into your daily routine, do it in the evening while you're watching TV or listening to music. Don't be a couch potato; get down on the floor and get flexible!

12. To help reduce muscle soreness after a strenuous ride, spin easily during the final 10 minutes and avoid hills.

13. When riding in icy windchills, apply a thin coat of petroleum jelly to exposed skin to prevent chapping.

14. Dressing in several light layers is the secret to taking the danger out of temperatures below freezing. Layers trap air to insulate against cold better than a single thick garment. Next to your skin, wear polypropylene, merino wool, or another fabric designed to wick away perspiration. You'll be drier and warmer. (Avoid cotton, which feels clammy when damp.) Add insulating layers of similar synthetics, and then cover it all with a breathable Windbreaker.

15. Don't overdress in cold weather. As a rule, you should feel a bit chilly during the initial mile. Pedaling will warm you up, but it won't cause you to start sweating.

16. A lightweight balaclava keeps you warmer all over because so much body heat is lost through the head and neck.

17. Control your body temperature by wearing a windbreaker with a full front zipper. Zip up when descending or riding into a head-wind; zip down when climbing or when the wind is behind you.

18. Wear a hydration pack on winter rides. It lets you carry extra supplies and get at them more easily than when they're in jersey pockets covered by your Windbreaker. The hydration pack also holds down the jacket so you can easily work the zipper with one hand to ventilate while riding. And it covers the small of your back to hold in body heat.

19. If you're going from sea level to high altitude (5,000 feet or more), expect your performance to suffer. The reason is not that there's less oxygen in the air; rather, the amount of atmospheric pressure forcing oxygen into your lungs is decreased. You get less oxygen from each breath, so your lungs and heart must work harder. The result can be breathing difficulty, fatigue, headache, and even nausea.

20. It takes about 3 weeks to acclimate to high altitude. The first week should be limited to easy rides, the second can include harder ones, and then the third is used to rest and recover. But what if you'll be riding at altitude for just 1 or 2 weeks? Keep all efforts aerobic, make frequent rest stops, eat plenty, and drink, drink, drink, to fend off dehydration. It's also important to protect your skin from the intense sunlight of higher elevations.

21. Here are a few ways to clean a water bottle or hydration bladder and reduce the plastic flavor.

- Fill the bottle or bladder with hot water and put in four drops of bleach. Let it stand overnight; then rinse with alternating hot and cold water to break the molecular surface tension of any remaining bleach. This kills bacteria and leaves no taste.

- If the idea of bleach doesn't appeal to you, use a teaspoon of lemon or lime juice. It won't kill bacteria, but it'll freshen the taste.

- Rinse the bottle or bladder with warm water containing a teaspoon of baking soda.

- Wash bottles in a dishwasher.

22. To stop that ugly green stuff from cropping up in your water bottles, rinse them after each ride, and then put them upside down in your bike's cages (with caps open) to drain and dry.

23. If you have a backpack-style hydration system, the damp reservoir and hose can become moldy if several days pass between uses. An easy way to prevent it is to blow out the hose, shake out the reservoir, and then toss them both into the freezer. Nothing can grow in there.

24. If you get something in your eye and your natural reflexes (blinking and tears) don't dispel it, stop and wash it out with water from your bottle. If no water is available, pull your upper eyelid over your lower one; then roll your eye. This often deposits the object on the lower lid.

25. Need a mirror for any reason, such as relocating a wayward contact lens or finding a gnat in your eye? There's one on the driver's-side door of every parked car.

26. Upon finishing a ride, brush your teeth before drinking and eating. Then you won't be washing down that film of saliva that's coated with the dust, grit, bugs, and other airborne stuff you've been breathing.

27. Don't apply alcohol to saddle sores or your crotch in general. It can dry the skin too much and cause additional irritation that leads to more sores.

28. To prevent numbness in the hands (ulnar neuropathy, or "handlebar palsy"), cushion the pressure points. This condition is caused

by compression of the nerves passing through the heel of the hand into the palm. Padded gloves and handlebar covers are helpful, as is a frequent change of grip on the bar.

29. Use this checklist to solve genital numbness, which is caused by saddle pressure on the two pudendal nerves in the crotch.

- **Is the saddle too far from the handlebar?** If you need to lean forward excessively to reach the bar, it makes the nose of the saddle press on the nerves. Install a shorter stem, or move the saddle forward if it won't adversely affect your pedaling position.

- **Is the nose of the saddle tipped up or down?** If up, it increases pressure as you lean forward. If down, you'll slide onto the narrow nose. Level the saddle by laying a yardstick along its length so you can compare it with a tabletop, a windowsill, or something else horizontal.

- **Is the saddle too high?** This will cause you to saw your crotch from side to side in order to reach the pedals. Lower the saddle until you can pedal backward smoothly, using your heels.

- **Is the saddle wide enough for sufficient support?** The rear portion must support your ischial tuberosities ("sit bones") to keep pressure off the tender tissue between them. A saddle that's too narrow or domed (when viewed from the rear) puts your sit bones over the sides instead of on top.

- **Is the saddle too soft?** A seat covered by a thick foam or gel padding isn't the solution to numbness. Instead, it actually exerts more pressure on your crotch as your sit bones sink in. Some padding is necessary for comfort, but too much is counterproductive.

- **Is the saddle up-to-date?** A number of recently designed seats have features that reduce the risk of genital numbness, including wedges or holes that remove material where it would contact the crotch. Some models are made specifically for

WAYS TO SCORE AGAINST SADDLE SORES

One of noncycling public's most pervasive misconceptions regarding cycling is that perching on a narrow racing saddle is tantamount to having your razor blades inserted under your toenails. In fact, proper equipment, apparel, and attention to the nether region can thwart almost any saddle-related ill. Read on.

1. **Dress right.** Wear shorts with a soft, absorbent, padded liner known as a chamois. Nowadays these are synthetic rather than leather, making shorts easier to care for. Some liners have an antibacterial treatment. Mountain bikers who shy away from tight Lycra can buy baggy shorts with sewn-in padded liners.

2. **Lubricate.** A cycling-specific skin conditioner, such as Assos Chamois Cream, all but eliminates the risk of chafing when it's applied before riding. Afterward, it washes away easily, making it superior to lubricants, like petroleum jelly, that clog pores and liners.

3. **Keep clean.** Wash your crotch and the shorts after every ride. Have at least two pairs of shorts so that one is always clean and ready.

4. **Be a quick-change artist.** Never hang around after a ride in your cycling shorts. The damp liner is a breeding ground for germs. Even if you can't wash right way, put on dry clothes next to your skin.

men, others for women. If you decide your present seat should be replaced, check into these anatomical models.

- **Are you standing enough?** During a long ride, periodically pedal out of the saddle for a minute to relieve pressure and restore circulation. This is particularly important if there aren't hills that make standing necessary or if you use an aero bar. It's common to lock into a low, forward position for minutes on end before realizing numbness is setting in.

5. Take your medication. Should a sore develop, treat it with an antibacterial wash and an antibiotic ointment. If you have more than an occasional small problem, ask a dermatologist for a prescription product such as erythromycin.

6. Avoid wearing tight pants when not riding. Loose clothing permits air circulation and helps keep you dry, thus inhibiting the growth of bacteria. Sleeping without underwear may also be helpful.

7. Be a smart rider. Stand when cycling over railroad tracks and rough patches, and make it a habit to pedal out of the saddle for about 1 minute in every 20. This restores blood and air circulation.

8. Assess your saddle. If your seat is too low, too high, or tilted up or down, this can cause excess crotch movement during pedaling and the broken skin that leads to sores.

9. Use a better seat. The same features that reduce numbness also limit the risk of saddle sores.

10. Give it a rest. If a saddle sore doesn't respond quickly to treatment, take a couple of days off the bike. Your butt and body can use the rest. In fact, slow-healing or recurring saddle sores are a sign of overtraining.

30. Saddles aren't the whole story when it comes to crotch comfort. Also important are cycling shorts with a soft, absorbent, padded liner. These are meant to be worn without underwear, by the way, to eliminate irritating seams.

31. If you're under 18 and suffer from leg muscle cramps when cycling, you may be pushing too hard for your age. Muscles don't mature until about age 18. Reduce the duration or intensity of rides just enough to eliminate cramping.

32. If you're suffering from Achilles tendon pain, try raising the saddle. This may seem to defy logic, but here's the thinking: With a lower saddle, you have a more horizontal foot position at the bottom of the pedal stroke. This puts more strain on the tendon because your ankle is bent at a right angle; your Achilles tendon and calf are stretched. Raising the saddle keeps your foot pointed slightly downward, reducing ankle movement.

33. Here's the rule of thumb for alleviating a sore knee: If it hurts in front, raise the saddle. If it hurts behind, lower the saddle.

34. If you're eating a normal diet and salting things lightly, you don't need salt tablets. Even when sweating off 2 pounds, you lose only 1 gram of sodium (the equivalent of 1/2 teaspoon of salt). Interestingly, because of decreased blood volume and the conservation of sodium by the kidneys, sodium concentration in the blood actually increases during exercise.

35. If you suffer from chondromalacia (a degeneration of the cartilage under the kneecap), cycling should help, not hurt, as long as you (1) adjust the saddle so your knee remains only slightly bent at the bottom of the pedal stroke, and (2) avoid big gears and long, steady, seated climbs. The key is to spin in moderate gears and stand for at least part of each hill.

36. Make sunscreen a part of your summer cycling kit. Most brands are rated numerically between 1 and 44 for their sun protection factor (SPF). The higher the number, the better they'll stop dangerous ultraviolet rays. Use a waterproof sunscreen so it won't be washed away by sweat. Apply it to your arms, legs, hands, face, and especially the back of your neck and ears. Don't forget behind your knees, a sensitive area that catches lots of sun.

37. Consider altering your riding schedule if the forecast high temperature (in Fahrenheit) plus the relative humidity adds up to 160 or more. For example, a temperature of 85 with 90 percent humidity equals 175. In such conditions, heat-related maladies become much more of a threat. You'd be smart to ride at daybreak or in late afternoon, avoiding the hottest part of the day.

38. To improve your performance, especially on hills, lose weight. The ideal amount of body fat for an elite cyclist is 6 to 9 percent for a man and 11 to 14 percent for a woman. Not everyone can reach those levels (or should even try to), but a performance-oriented cyclist must do better than the 20 and 25 percent body fat found in the average adult male and female, respectively.

39. Percentage of body fat can't be determined with a bathroom scale. You need to have it calculated by a professional using one of three common methods: underwater weighing, skinfold measurement, or electrical impedance. To have yourself measured, check local hospitals, athletic clubs, college physiology departments, or sports medicine physicians.

40. A good way to determine your personal fluid needs is to weigh yourself before and after a hot-weather, long-distance ride. Remember that a pint of water equals 1 pound. If your weight drops more than 2 pounds during the ride, increase your fluid intake proportionately.

41. The patella tendon, which attaches the kneecap to the shinbone, is crucial for pedaling because the entire force of the quadriceps contraction is dependent on its strength. This is why the tendon is occasionally injured. Therapy includes ice massage, anti-inflammatory medication, and quadriceps exercises such as straight leg raises in multiple directions. To recover fully, you need to avoid squatting, kneeling, going up and down stairs, and exercising on knee extension machines. On the bike, raise your saddle slightly and spin against a low resistance.

42. Dehydration is a big risk in cold weather, but water freezes quickly. To keep it drinkable, start with it warm and carry it in an insulated case. Put your second bottle in a jersey pocket under your Windbreaker. You could also invest in a winter hydration pack with an insulated drinking tube.

43. Saltwater freezes at a lower temperature than plain water. To help keep the large volume of water in a backpack-style hydration system from icing up, add a teaspoon of salt when you fill it.

44. If you tend to get earaches when riding in cool or windy weather, put cotton in your ears. Also, don't clean your ears with swabs or drops. Removing the wax makes them more vulnerable to the rushing air.

45. To minimize danger from carbon monoxide in the air, it makes sense to avoid roads with heavy traffic. Even worse are busy roads that are lined with trees. A study found that overhanging limbs can trap dangerous levels of carbon monoxide. Realize, too, that the problem is greater in winter because cold engines produce higher concentrations of the gas.

46. If cycling makes your nose run similar to having a cold or allergy, you're probably suffering from a condition called vasomotor rhinitis. It's believed to be caused by an imbalance of nerve impulses to the nose. This results in overactive parasympathetic nerves, which are responsible for nasal secretion. Relief usually comes with a prescription drug known as ipatropium (Atrovent).

47. Don't drink from another person's water bottle. This practice can spread colds or ailments much worse. Enteroviral infections are carried by fluids and have caused outbreaks of diseases such as aseptic meningitis.

48. If you have varicose veins, it's possible that cycling could worsen the condition unless you take precautions. The risk is from the buildup of venous pressure caused by pedaling. In addition, the bent-over riding position can impede bloodflow from the legs to the heart. To counteract these potential problems, rest with your legs elevated above heart level after riding and at the end of the day. Walking after a ride is helpful, too.

49. Wear your sunglasses even on cloudy days. In fact, your eyes are more at risk from ultraviolet sun rays when it's overcast because they lose the natural protection that stems from squinting and increased blinking.

50. On long rides (over 2 hours), you must replace electrolytes. These are minerals (such as sodium, chloride, and potassium) that carry an electrical charge that's necessary for muscle contraction and the maintenance of fluid levels. If you don't use a sports drink (or don't eat) on an extended ride, you can suffer electrolyte imbalances such as a low-sodium condition called hyponatremia. This results in lethargy, muscle weakness, and confusion.

51. There are several good reasons that serious male cyclists traditionally shave their legs. One is to provide a smooth working surface for massage. Another is ease of treating crash rash. If legs are already shaved, hair won't have to be removed before bandaging. Plus, hair won't be matted in the wound, which reduces the chance of infection. Some evidence even suggests that smooth skin slides better, thus reducing the severity of abrasions. Hairless skin is also more aerodynamic and—admit it, guys— shaving helps leg muscles pop.

52. For first-time leg shavers, don't wait until the eve of a big event. The strange feel of the bedsheets can disrupt sleep. Use electric clippers for the initial denuding, then a razor and shaving cream to attack the stubble. A weekly once-over in the shower will keep you slick for the rest of the season.

53. Crash rash isn't a rash at all. It's a common cycling injury in which outer layers of skin are scraped away as a result of sliding over a rough, gritty surface. This exposes deeper layers and damages blood vessels, which ooze and create the familiar red badge. Follow these six tips to treat it.

- Quickly get to a place where you can thoroughly clean and disinfect the wound. It is less painful if done within 30 minutes of the crash because nerve endings are still numb from the trauma.

- To prevent infection and scarring, scrub the wound hard with a rough washcloth or a medium/soft-bristle brush. Apply a liberal amount of an antibacterial surgical soap such as Hibiclens or Betadine.

- Pat the wound dry; then apply an antibacterial ointment such as Neosporin (which, along with the products mentioned above, is available, without a prescription, at drugstores).

- Cover the cleaned abrasion with a nonstick sterile dressing such as Telfa or Second Skin. To prevent it from leaking onto clothes or sheets, cover the dressing with a layer of absorbent gauze for the first few days.

- Change the dressing each morning and night. Apply more antibacterial ointment before covering the wound, and check for signs of infection: tenderness, swollen red skin, sensation of heat. If you detect any of these, consult a doctor.

- To minimize scarring, keep the wound moist so a hard scab can't develop. As new skin starts to form, apply Saratoga ointment and light gauze. This zinc oxide-based salve prevents scabbing. Then use a moisturizer on new skin for at least a week.

54. For upper-body protection against crash rash, wear a T-shirt under your cycling jersey. This lets the outer garment slide against the inner one instead of your skin, reducing abrasions.

55. Make sure your tetanus vaccination is current. If you should crash and suffer cuts or abrasions and it's been several years since your last tetanus shot, get one within 24 hours. Tetanus bacteria produce powerful toxins, so don't treat the risk lightly.

56. The hazards of consuming more than 2 ounces of alcohol per day are well-known, and here's another one: It can hurt your cycling

performance by disturbing your body's delicate balance of iron and other vital elements. It also increases fluid loss through urination, which can cause dehydration. In fact, your body needs 8 ounces of water to metabolize 1 ounce of alcohol.

57. If you party hard on Friday night, don't expect to ride well again until Sunday. Studies show that it takes at least 36 hours before the performance-impairing effects of alcohol wear off.

58. Insufficient sleep won't necessarily hurt your cycling. Researchers have found that strength, aerobic ability, and heart rate don't change significantly even after 60 hours of sleep deprivation. What does change are mood and perception. On long rides, this may reduce performance.

59. Take precautions to avoid catching a cold, which can set back your training by a week or more. Most colds aren't spread by coughing or sneezing but by hand contact. During cold season, wash your hands several times daily, and avoid touching your mouth, eyes, or nose until after you do.

60. Stay off the bike during the two or three (on average) colds you'll catch each year. If you must ride, take it easy because viruses often travel to muscles, where they cause microscopic damage and fatigue. In fact, a 15 percent loss of strength has been found among people who recently had a virus.

61. If weight loss is your goal, select the gears in which you can generate the fastest speed for the time you're riding. Contrary to the popular theory that low-intensity exercise causes the body to burn more stored fat for energy, don't restrict your effort. It's total calorie consumption that's most important. The harder you ride for any given period, the more calories you burn.

62. To lose weight at a safe rate of 1 pound per week, eat 3,500 calories less than you expend. Most fast recreational cyclists burn around 500 calories per hour of riding.

63. Have a sore knee or muscle? There's an easy way to apply cold after rides. Just keep a large bag of frozen corn or peas in the freezer. Lay it on the hurt for about 10 minutes. It's as effective as using ice, but quicker and drier.

64. For a handy way to do ice massage, fill some 3-ounce bathroom cups about three-quarters full with water and store them in your freezer. Peel back the paper so you can rub with the ice end while you hold the paper end.

65. If your cleats and saddle are properly adjusted, knee noises aren't anything to worry about unless they're accompanied by pain.

66. The sound your sore knees make may provide a clue to the problem. Popping indicates osteoarthritis, whereas a noise like hook-and-loop material pulling apart suggests rheumatoid arthritis. A healthy knee sounds like a well-oiled seesaw.

67. If you suffer from lower-back pain linked to riding, you may have a strength imbalance between your stomach muscles and those that lift your legs. A cure may be as simple as a daily dose of crunches. To do them, lie on your back with your knees bent 90 degrees and your hands on your chest. Roll your shoulders forward; then pause for a moment just before the small of your back leaves the floor, as shown in the photo. Lower slowly and repeat. Start with 20, and add more as your abdominal strength increases.

68. An occasional bout of dizziness, especially when you stand up quickly, is usually nothing to be alarmed about. It's probably the onset of vasovagal syncope, a condition that occurs when your blood pressure is temporariiy too iow to get enough blood to your brain. It's common in people with slow pulse rates and low blood pressure. In other words, fit cyclists. If you feel it happening, bend over or lie down. The black spots will disappear in a few seconds.

69. Keep riding to improve your cholesterol and thereby lower your risk of heart disease. It's been found that people who ride 1 hour a day, four or five times per week, experience an average 13 per-

cent increase in their HDL, the "good" cholesterol that counter-acts the harmful, LDL type. This translates to a 10 to 20 percent reduction in the risk of heart disease.

70. If your saddle height seems correct for only one leg because the other is reaching for the pedal, you may have a significant leg-length discrepancy. For a quick check, remove your shoes and socks, lie on your back, and then have a friend pick up your legs by the heels and shake them gently. When they're laid down to-gether, your friend will be able to judge if one leg seems longer.

71. Ignore a leg-length discrepancy of ⅛ inch or less. But if it seems more, see your doctor to get what's known as a scanogram x-ray. This is done with a measuring stick beside your leg, enabling a precise measurement of the bones.

72. If your leg-length discrepancy is ⅛ to ⅜ inch, correct the differ-ence even if you're not experiencing problems. They might be just around the corner as you continue to ride with this imbal-ance. The correction is made at the ball of the foot, not the heel (as for runners), because this is where you contact the pedal. A discrepancy of up to ⅜ inch can be corrected by using a thicker

or double insole in the shoe of the shorter leg. Or slide the cleat of your longer leg rearward about ⅜ inch. For larger discrepancies, raise your shorter leg by placing a hard rubber or plastic block between the cleat and the shoe. It's best to combine the different remedies so you don't radically modify pedal position or the fit of your shoes. It's difficult and unnecessary to precisely correct the full amount of a large discrepancy. Just get within 75 percent.

73. If you experience pain along the outside of your knee, it's likely to be iliotibial band (ITB) friction syndrome. This condition arises when the fibrous band on the outside of your upper leg rubs against the knee's bony protrusion. It can result from improper cleat position, low seat height, bowed legs, wide hips, or a change in riding position. In some cases it's just a matter of riding more than you're ready for yet. The remedy is ice, massage, anti-inflammatory medications such as aspirin, ibuprofen or naproxen, and/or a better riding position. Some time off the bike may also be in order. If ignored, ITB syndrome can become severe enough to require surgery.

74. Inhaling frigid air during winter rides will not damage your throat or lungs. Exercise markedly increases body temperature, and the extra heat you generate instantly warms each breath you take.

75. Keep riding as you age if you want a better quality of life. Research has found that older adults who exercise regularly have sharper minds than those who don't. In one study, the active group scored higher in tests for reasoning, memory, vocabulary, and reaction time.

76. Men needn't worry that cycling can somehow result in prostate cancer. There's no known connection. However, some doctors contend that cycling may aggravate prostatitis (an inflammation of the prostate gland, located at the base of the urethra).

77. If you have high blood pressure, think twice about riding after you've consumed caffeine. It's been shown that the caffeine equivalent of two cups of coffee, when combined with exercise, can result in blood pressure readings twice as high as those produced by exercise alone.

78. Relieve foot discomfort by occasionally not pushing down for several strokes. By your only pulling up, pressure is reduced on your soles and circulation is restored.

79. If you sometimes feel nauseated when riding, here are some possible causes and solutions.

- **Slow gastric emptying.** When you ride with food or fluid in your belly, the stomach and working muscles battle for extra blood. The muscles always win, so food sits and makes you feel sick. *Solution:* There will be less risk if you don't ride hard after eating and you gradually condition your system to digest food during cycling.

- **Aggravated stomach lining.** When liquid sloshes in your stomach, its mucous membrane can become irritated. *Solution:* Don't drink while riding on bouncy surfaces.

- **Lowered pH.** Vigorous riding exhausts the fuel in muscle cells and produces acids. If the level of exercise is so high that your body is unable to buffer these acids, your pH level will fall, triggering nausea, headache, restlessness, and weakness. *Solution:* Back off your effort at the first sign of stomach distress.

- **Dehydration.** If you're riding in hot weather and don't drink enough, you could become nauseated. And once your stomach is upset, you won't want to put anything in it, so the problem is compounded. *Solution:* Drink early and often on every ride.

- **Anxiety.** Pre-event butterflies can stress your system just as much as high-intensity exercise and heat. *Solution:* If you tend to get this nervous, eat only easily digestible foods, and do it about 3 hours before the start.

58 TIPS FOR BETTER NUTRITION

If you're not confused about nutrition, you're not human. One day, it's high carb, low fat; the next, it's low carb, high protein. But no matter the diet du jour, cyclists can revel in one, simple fact: Because cycling burns so many calories, you're earning some leniency concerning your diet. That doesn't mean you should start ordering Ben & Jerry's by the case, but it does mean you should stop feeling guilty every time you pick up a spoon. The following tips will go even further to ensure you fuel your body properly (and tastily!).

1. If you remember only one rule about on-bike nutrition, remember this one: Drink before you're thirsty, eat before you're hungry.

2. Never experiment with foods, drinks, or eating patterns on an important ride. Do it during training to find out what works and what doesn't.

3. When mixing a powdered sports drink, put a less concentrated solution into the bottle(s) you'll drink last. Drinks always taste sweeter the longer you ride. What seems pleasant initially can taste syrupy 3 hours later.

4. Drink more than you think you need to. If you become thirsty during a ride, you've made a big mistake. In hot weather, you should be downing the better part of two bottles per hour. Why so much? Dehydration is one of the primary—but most easily avoided—contributors to fatigue.

5. If your watch has a countdown timer, set it for 10-minute intervals. Each beep then becomes a reminder to take a swig from your bottle.

6. When the temperature makes full-finger gloves necessary, un-wrap, slice, and repackage your snacks. This makes it much easier to grab a bite-size morsel while cycling.

7. If you're interested in losing a few pounds, schedule your rides for midday. Not only will you burn calories, but the exercise will sup-press your appetite. Afterward, you'll be satisfied with a low-calorie lunch consisting of a piece of fruit and a cup of fat-free yogurt.

8. The most nutritious fast foods are Chinese, Mexican, and Italian. If chosen wisely, they can have less fat and more energy-yielding carbohydrate than other cuisine. Of course, any fast food will be tend to be higher in fat and sodium than is good for you.

9. Do not get swept up in the low-carb diet craze. The best fuel for cycling is complex carbohydrate as found in grains, fruit, potatoes, vegetables, cereals, pasta, and bread. As opposed to simple or re-fined carbohydrate like sugar, candy, and soda, the complex kind supplies vitamins, minerals, and fiber. Once digested, carbohy-drate is stored in the muscles and liver as glycogen. This is the pri-mary fuel for intense efforts such as sprinting and fast climbing.

10. At least 60 percent of your total daily calories should be in the form of complex carbohydrate. During the first 24 hours after an exhausting ride, there's no difference in the synthesis of glycogen between complex and simple carbohydrate. But after a day, com-plex carbo promotes a significantly greater amount.

11. If you ride more than 2 hours per day, increase your intake of complex carbo from 60 to 70 percent.

12. Freeze your liquids for hot rides. They'll slowly thaw and supply you with cool refreshment. Conversely, start cold rides with hot liquids. In very cold weather, fill your bottle or hydration system with hot water to prevent icing.

13. Make your own carbohydrate drink with equal parts water and fruit juice. Apple and grape are popular. Beware of citrus juices, which can be harsh on an active stomach.

CALORIES BURNED

Speed (mph)	Calories/min	Calories/mi
22.5	24.0	64.0
21.0	19.5	55.7
18.5	15.0	48.6
16.0	19.5	39.3
12.0	6.0	30.0
8.3	3.75	27.0
6.0	2.65	26.5

14. For optimal cooling and hydration, drink plenty before a ride, not just during it. Consume about 16 ounces of water 1 to 2 hours before departing, and another 10 to 16 ounces with about 20 minutes to go.

15. Nibble solid food almost continuously during long rides. Good choices are foods high in carbohydrate that are also easy to digest, such as fruit, cookies, and bagels. A more high-tech answer is energy bars, which come in many flavors and usually contain more than 200 calories, along with a variety of nutrients.

16. To lose 1 pound of body fat per week, burn approximately 3,500 more calories than you eat. Use the table to estimate calorie consumption during a ride.

17. Caffeine can help your body tap the energy contained in stored fat, thereby conserving your primary muscle fuel, glycogen. Caffeine is a drug that some people don't tolerate well, however. It can cause nervousness, upset stomach, and increased urination, which increases the risk of dehydration. Be careful if you don't normally drink coffee or other caffeinated beverages.

18. On a very long ride, eat your food in this order: (1) sandwiches that contain meat or high-fat items such as peanut butter or cream cheese; (2) fruit, cookies, jam sandwiches, energy bars, and other complex carbohydrates; (3) simple sugars in the form of carbo gels or dextrose, glucose, or fructose wafers. This sequence is advocated by former U.S. national team coach Eddie Borysewicz, who says it gives you time-released fuel. As the first foods are slowly being digested to supply food energy for the end of the ride, the faster-digesting second and third foods are at work. In addition, begin sipping a sports drink right from the start to help keep blood glucose levels high.

19. To prevent the "bonk" (hypoglycemia)—which is marked by tiredness, irritability, dizziness, confusion, and sometimes nausea—don't allow your blood glucose to become depleted. Blood glucose is the sole substance that fuels the brain and central nervous system. It's derived from the same carbohydrate-rich foods and drinks that produce the muscle fuel glycogen.

20. Once you start bonking, immediately drink something rich in carbohydrate. You can rebound from the bonk, but when you "hit the wall" you're essentially done for the day. This term describes the impact when muscle glycogen is exhausted. Only rest and digestion of high-carbo foods can bring you back, and these things take time.

21. Diet in winter, not summer. Don't try to cut calories when you're riding nearly every day and doing distance on weekends. You'll lose strength and ambition as surely as you lose weight.

22. When you're eating while riding, choking is a danger. It helps to clear your nose first so you can breathe freely as you chew. Take small bites, and don't swallow until the food is thoroughly ground up. This also aids digestion.

23. Make it easier to eat on the bike by cutting foods into bite-size pieces and putting them into plastic bags. Quarter your sandwiches. Slice your apples. Peel and divide your orange segments. Dates and dried apricots are just the right size. So are fig bars.

24. Your body's balance of electrolytes (the minerals sodium, potassium, and chloride) is important because a disruption can result in decreased performance, cramps, and heat stroke during hot-weather rides beyond 2 hours. Fortunately, electrolytes are easily replenished by swigging most sports drinks (check the label) or eating fruits or vegetables.

25. When riding one-handed so you can reach back into your jersey pockets, grip a drop handlebar next to the stem. This helps you sit up, and your movements won't be as likely to make the bike swerve.

26. When riding in a paceline, wait until you're at the rear to do your drinking or eating. Then you won't be a danger to the other riders if you don't hold a straight line.

27. Before a race or other hard ride, follow these rules.

   • Eat a big enough meal 2 to 3 hours beforehand to keep from feeling hungry at the start and during the first hour.

   • Base the meal on easily digested complex carbohydrate (grains, fruit, potatoes, pasta, bread) so your upper intestinal tract is empty by event time. This helps prevent the cramping that can result from competition between your muscles and digestive system for a blood supply.

   • Drink plenty of fluids with the meal. A good choice is one that provides calories and electrolytes, such as fruit juice or a sports drink.

28. For a preride breakfast, try these racer favorites: rice pudding (212 calories per serving), fat-free yogurt (114 per cup), muffins (103 calories each), whole wheat toast (59 calories per slice), oatmeal (145 calories per cup), whole grain cereal (111 calories per serving).

29. At breakfast before an epic road or mountain bike ride, include some protein and fat with your carbohydrate foods. For example, have a cheese omelette with your pancakes. Many riders find that the protein and fat extends a meal's "burn time." They don't

get that hollow feeling in their stomachs as soon as when eating only carbo.

30. It's okay to eat breakfast close to your start time when you're taking a long recreational ride. The early pace can be easy, allowing digestion on the bike. Even so, begin nibbling during the first 90 minutes; then keep it up.

31. Don't attempt to build an energy-rich carbohydrate reserve by eating large quantities at the pre-event meal. That meal is only for topping off your tank. It takes 12 to 24 hours to digest and store carbohydrate as glycogen. Put the emphasis on pasta, rice,

7 WAYS TO ELIMINATE FAT

The bad news: Weight gain is a sneaky thing, always lurking in the shadows of empty potato chip bags and ice cream cartons. The good news: It's not hard to stay one step ahead of excess baggage. Here are seven painless methods.

1. Keep a food diary along with your training diary. Look for things that disrupt good nutrition or a steady intake of calories throughout the day.

2. Replace bad foods with good ones. Eat less calorically dense fat while eating more complex carbohydrate.

3. Don't skip meals. In fact, add one or two, and decrease the amount you eat in the standard three.

4. Decrease high-calorie portions. Enjoy fun foods like pizza, ice cream, or cookies, but do it in moderation.

5. Don't deprive yourself of foods you crave. Reward yourself on special occasions, such as after your longest ride of the week.

6. Don't starve yourself. If you overeat one day, don't fast the next day to compensate. Simply accept the transgression and start anew the morning after.

7. Ride more. It's a great way to lose weight if you find it too tough to significantly decrease your calorie consumption.

potatoes, bread, vegetables, and other complex carbo during the 2 or 3 days leading up to the event.

32. Don't eat solid food during the 30 minutes before a substantial climb. It won't digest fast enough to give you energy, and it may upset your stomach when the pedaling gets strenuous.

33. For short workouts, it's better not to eat beforehand. Otherwise, some of your blood will be used for digestion rather than for supplying oxygen and nutrients to your working muscles. Your legs don't need to be fed—they have enough stored glycogen for an hour-long ride.

34. Remember this rule of endurance cycling: You can ride well 2½ hours without eating. But if you do eat, you can ride well all day.

35. Bananas supply about 100 calories each, plus potassium—an important electrolyte for warding off muscle cramps. In addition, bananas come with a built-in wrapper. Peel only as much as you want to eat; then slip what's left into a rear jersey pocket. Leave some peel hanging over the edge so it's easy to grab.

36. You needn't be too choosy when selecting a sports drink. The type of simple sugar used in them doesn't seem to matter and is probably outweighed by other factors, such as flavor. If you like the taste, you're likely to drink more.

37. If certain energy bars or drinks don't seem to agree with you, check the ingredients. The simple sugar called fructose can cause stomach upset in some people. Try products that use a different sweetener to see if you feel better.

38. Because you'll burn 3,000 to 5,000 calories per day on an extended tour, it's a great chance to eat as much as you want. But this isn't a license to pedal from one fast-food joint to the next. Instead, maintain your sensible cycling ratios of 60 percent carbohydrate, 25 to 30 percent fat, and 10 to 15 percent protein.

39. Think twice about drinking tea or coffee with meals. The tannic acid they contain inhibits the rate of absorption of iron by 50 percent. A low iron level is one of the most common deficiencies in the American diet. Iron is essential for the quantity and quality of red blood cells, which deliver oxygen to muscles and tissues, so a deficiency can hurt cycling performance.

40. If you eat pasta before a big event, you'll be in the company of 83 percent of world-class cyclists, according to one poll. Their pasta of choice is spaghetti, and 60 percent of them eat it at least three times per week. Some favorites of the pros: pasta topped with honey, cold spaghetti with cottage cheese and cinnamon sugar, and pasta smothered with peanut butter.

41. If you find yourself falling prey to binge eating, it may be a sign of overtraining. When you ride too much without adequate recovery, your muscle tissue can break down faster than your body can replace it. This causes an imbalance in the level of tryptophan, an amino acid that influences brain serotonin levels. Serotonin, in turn, regulates mood, pain sensitivity, and sleep. A lack of it may also produce carbohydrate cravings. This could be what's happening if you find it difficult to stop eating.

42. Eat five small meals each day, instead of two or three big ones. Small meals spread calories throughout the day, providing a continuous source of energy. Processing a large meal can actually sap energy. Also, when you overload your digestive system, your body can't efficiently process all the calories. Some are diverted into fat stores.

43. If you're trying to lose weight, here are some ways to maximize the number of calories you burn on a ride.

- **Head for the hills.** Climbing at any speed consumes more calories than cycling on flat ground at the same rate. Descents won't cancel this extra expenditure, especially if you pedal instead of coast.

- **Ride when it's windy.** On a loop or an out-and-back course, the energy saved with a tailwind doesn't offset the extra calories burned against a headwind.

- **Sit up.** At speeds greater than 15 mph, an upright riding position results in significantly more calories burned than a low position, which reduces wind resistance.

- **Leave your rack, bags, and fenders on.** Anything that adds weight or wind resistance makes you use more energy. You won't just get lighter; you'll get stronger.

- **Don't draft.** Riding in the slipstream of another rider reduces your workload by about 1 percent for each mile per hour.

44. In the latter stages of a long ride, visions of high-fat foods may start dancing in your head. Don't succumb to these cravings if you make a convenience store stop. Things like chips and nuts are not efficient fuel. They take longer to digest, which creates competition between your stomach and muscles for a blood supply. In the end your muscles will win, and your stomach may be a sore loser.

45. In most cases there's no need to consume water if you're using a sports drink. Studies show that although sports drinks do empty from the stomach slower than water, they're processed faster by the intestines. Thus, there's no difference in the rate at which these fluids enter the bloodstream.

46. Tired of pasta? Try these two non-Italian cuisines that supply ample amounts of energy-producing carbohydrate.

- Asian. The major ingredients in Chinese food (rice, noodles, and vegetables) are rich in carbo. Small amounts of meat and fish are also used in many dishes. This combination offers the right proportion of carbohydrate to protein and fat. Meals from Thailand, Korea, Vietnam, and India feature beans, rice, grains, vegetables, and breads, all of which are good sources of complex carbo.

- Mexican. Tortillas, enchiladas, and chili (non-carne) are all fine carbo dishes. Just be sure to limit fried or refried dishes (they contain more fat) and those that are full of meat or cheese.

47. The process of carbohydrate loading used to be a week-long process of energy depletion and refueling. It was complicated and not much fun. Now we know that cyclists can do just as well simply by increasing carbo intake during the 3 days before an important long or high-intensity event. Combined with tapering your training, this leaves your body rested and your muscles brimming with glycogen. Be sure to drink plenty of liquids during this period—necessary for carbo metabolism and pre-event hydration.

48. If you're unfit, don't bother to carbo-load. Your muscles won't store more than their usual amount of glycogen, and the extra carbohydrate calories will be converted to fat. You wouldn't put jet fuel in a minivan, would you?

49. If your legs feel stiff and thick after carbo-loading, don't worry. This is normal because high levels of glycogen cause fluid retention in muscles. Once you start lowering glycogen levels during the warmup and the event itself, the heaviness will disappear.

50. Shortly after a ride of more than 2½ hours, which will deplete your glycogen stores, be sure to down high-carbohydrate foods or drinks. This brief postride period, known as the glycogen window, is when your muscles are most receptive to refueling. By using it then, you'll recover faster and feel stronger the next day. Be prompt because the window gradually closes after the first hour.

51. When you're on a long ride and need to stop at a convenience store for food, here are the best choices to choose to maintain a

8 FIXES FOR WINTER WEIGHT GAIN ⟩⟩⟩

Holiday buffets. Snow. Rain. Cold. Winter can seem like a cruel conspiracy to cyclists struggling to keep their weight in check. But it needn't be that way, not if you follow the guidelines below.

1. Eat less, but more often. Getting most of your daily calories from a single meal (especially at dinner, close to bedtime) overloads your system and contributes to weight gain.

2. Monitor your weight. If it increases each winter and decreases every spring, the extra pounds will gradually become easier to regain and harder to shed.

3. Avoid "heavy" foods. These include creamy sauces, dressings, and all saturated fats—fare that's everywhere during the winter holidays.

4. Keep riding. Less saddle time is the most obvious reason for gaining winter weight. If it's too cold or snowy outside, use an indoor trainer or rollers.

5. Try other sports. An ideal alternative is swimming. It's a whole-body exercise that burns plenty of calories, and there's minimal risk of injury. Cross-country skiing is an excellent way to work out in your endurance and interval zones while working your whole body.

6. Don't eat so much. It's as simple as that. Weight gain is caused by eating more calories than you burn.

7. Don't freak out if you gain a few pounds. Cycling is one of the best-ever weight-loss sports, and as you begin riding regularly in the spring, the pounds will melt with the snow.

8. If riding a trainer alone bores you to tears, sign up for group Spinning classes at a local gym. It's a social and very productive workout.

good cycling ratio of 60 percent carbohydrate and less than 30 percent fat.

- **Energy bars.** Even the smallest convenience stores now stock an assortment of energy bars. You might not find your favorite brand, but chances are you will find at least one type of high-carb, high-protein, low-fat treat.

- **Snack items:** The best choice is a bag of pretzels (low salt, if possible). Unlike chips or nuts, pretzels aren't high in fat. An ounce of pretzel sticks has about 110 calories, 81 percent from carbohydrate.

- **Cookies:** Fig bars have long been the standard for cyclists. Each one has about 50 calories, 83 percent from carbohydrate. Nowadays you'll find many other varieties of low-fat or fat-free cookies, too.

- **Candy bars:** Most have an unacceptable 1:1 ratio of fat to carbohydrate. The exceptions are Milky Way, which is 66 percent carbohydrate and provides 260 calories, and 3 Musketeers, which has 250 calories but only 6 grams of fat.

- **Pastries:** Believe it or not, the best choice in this category may be that old junk food standard, Twinkies. Two of them provide 286 calories, of which 68 percent come from carbohydrate and only 26 percent from fat.

- **Ice cream and yogurt:** Of the 167 calories in an ice cream sandwich, nearly two-thirds come from carbohydrate. Yogurt is even better. A cup of fruit-flavored low-fat yogurt (225 calories) is 75 percent carbohydrate and only 10 percent fat.

- **Cold drinks:** Sports drinks are the best choice. Even small stores now stock the national brands. All their calories are carbohydrate, and most brands give you back some of the potassium and sodium lost in sweat.

- **Fruit:** For healthful nutrition, this is the best choice of all. Fruit is nearly 100 percent carbohydrate and a good provider of vitamins, minerals, and fiber. A banana supplies 100 calories, an apple about 80 calories, and an orange about 60 calories.

52. When planning a midride break at a fast-food restaurant, choose one that offers pizza or Mexican. Three slices of a 12-inch cheese pizza give you 650 calories, of which 59 percent are carbohydrate and just 17 percent are fat. A bean tostado (179 calories), an order of beans and cheese (232 calories), or a bean burrito (350 calories) is more than 50 percent carbohydrate and less than 30 percent fat.

53. Don't bother taking vitamin supplements, scientists say, if you're doing it for improved performance. Vitamins do not provide calories or a direct source of energy. They are helpful, however, if you have a nutritional deficiency or certain medical conditions.

54. Instead of taking expensive amino acid supplements, get all the aminos you need by eating protein-rich foods such as chicken, fish, and dairy products. The claim that amino acid supplements increase muscle mass and decrease body fat remains unproven.

55. Drinking beer is a poor way to carbo-load. One bottle (12 ounces) provides a scant 50 calories of carbohydrate. Wine is even weaker. A 4-ounce glass contains just 15 carbo calories. The poorest carbo-loader, however, is liquor, which has no carbohydrate at all. In addition, alcohol in any form is a diuretic, making it more difficult to stay properly hydrated.

56. Having a healthful diet doesn't mean avoiding fatty foods altogether. Enjoy them occasionally if you have a craving. There may be some truth to the contention that your body knows what it needs. Once satisfied, return to eating the low-fat foods that are the foundation of sound nutrition.

57. If you're trying to decide between fruit and fruit juice to carry on a ride, you're better off taking both. Juices have about twice the water content of whole fruits, which helps limit the chance of dehydration. However, juices contain negligible amounts of dietary fiber. Whole fruits have lots of it, which is why they're more filling. In terms of carbohydrate calories, 1/2 cup of any fruit juice provides approximately 60, only slightly less than a medium-size piece of fruit.

58. During hot summer rides, keep your on-bike drinks cold by starting with frozen bottles, using ice cubes, or using insulated bottles or covers. Temperature plays a role not only in a drink's taste but also in its effectiveness. A cold beverage is refreshing, and studies have shown that it lowers core body temperature. Plus, it digests and goes to work faster than a warm drink.

7

31 TIPS FOR BETTER EQUIPMENT

Stuff. Cycling's full of it. From apparel to components, to frames and forks, it's a world besieged by equipment. And while you needn't know it all (that's what your local shop is for), it's important to have a good handle on the basics. The following tips will help you understand how stuff can work for you.

1. Installing lighter inner tubes is an economical way to improve your bike's performance. This is because wheel weight has a profound effect on acceleration and speed. An ultralight tube may weigh half as much as a standard one yet cost only $2 to $4 more. That's a bargain compared with the cost of reducing wheel weight by replacing tires, rims, or spokes.

2. It's best to have two air pumps: a floor model for home use and a portable one for emergencies. A frame-mount pump or minipump won't last long if used frequently for routine inflation, so save it for when you have no other option.

3. Women, particularly those who are 5 foot 4 or shorter, should consider a specially designed bike. Many companies make models that are built for the female anatomy. A typical woman has a shorter torso and arms, but longer legs, than a man of the same height. She also has narrower shoulders, smaller hands and feet, and a wider pelvis. All of these things combine to make it difficult for many women to obtain a comfortable, efficient riding position on a bike with standard dimensions and components.

4. If you ride much at night, consider a lighting system that has a rechargeable battery pack. You'll pay more initially, but save in the long run by not having to buy batteries. The light beam is also much brighter.

5. Always have at least one rear reflector on your bike for times when you get caught out at dusk. If you ride at night, install a battery-powered red rear light, preferably a flashing one.

6. The best place for reflectors is on the rear of your pedals. The up-and-down motion is very effective at catching motorists' attention. If your pedals won't accept bolt-on reflectors, use reflective tape or wear reflective ankle bands.

7. Install a rear rack and an expandable trunk that sits on top. Then use your bike for short errands. This keeps you and your car in better shape. The trunk can carry items you need to take places or bring back. A rack that clamps onto your seat tube with a quick-release mechanism turns a racing bike into a commuter in an instant.

NEW BIKE CHECKLIST ≫≫≫

So you're buying a new bike? Congratulations! Here are nine things to remember when you go to the store to pick it up.

1. Make sure it's the exact model, color, and size you want. Be sure components were exchanged or accessories installed as you ordered.

2. Have your riding clothes and shoes so it's easy to accurately adjust the seat and handlebar. If you use a particular type of clipless pedal, bring your pedals as well.

3. Spin the wheels to make sure they're true and the brakes don't rub.

4. Be sure the tires are inflated to the manufacturer's recommended pressure.

5. If you're uncertain, ask how the quick-releases work on the brakes and hubs. Remove and reinstall a wheel several times to become familiar with the procedure.

6. Learn how to remove slack from the gear and brake cables, using the barrel adjusters.

7. Before heading for home, go for a short test ride to make sure everything is working properly.

8. Ask about the free 30-day checkup that most shops provide, and don't forget the owner's manual. Read it thoroughly prior to your first real ride.

9. If you're buying a new mountain bike, it almost certainly has suspension. Be sure the shop sets the suspension to your weight and riding style, and have them show you how to make adjustments yourself.

8. If you have smooth-tread tires on your road bike and the rear one slips on climbs, try substituting a treaded model. But a better—and less costly—solution is to keep your weight low and shift it rearward as you would to improve off-road climbing traction on a mountain bike.

9. Buy a tire with a Kevlar bead if you want to carry a spare in your toolbox or in your panniers on a tour. Kevlar beads can be folded without damage, but conventional wire beads can't. The metal will kink, and this could lead to a sidewall blowout.

10. Base your mountain bike tire selection on the ground conditions in your area. There's a big variety of tread designs and widths. Some work especially well on firm surfaces, whereas others excel on soft, wet soil. If your present tires don't have the traction or speed you need, ask experienced local riders and shop mechanics for their recommendations.

11. If your present saddle is a pain in the, uh . . . a source of discomfort, it's probably too narrow to fully support your ischial tuberosities ("sit bones"). It might also have inadequate padding, or it may have too much. Extra-thick foam or gel can exert excess pressure in the center as your sit bones sink into the sides.

12. Because women typically have a wider distance between their sit bones than men do, standard saddles may not be comfortable. Several companies make seats that are both wider and shorter to more naturally accommodate a woman's anatomy.

13. Use these tips if you live in a region with lots of rainy weather.

- Wear yellow or orange on dank days to be more visible to motorists.

- Put a cap under your helmet or attach a visor to shield your eyes.

- Install lightweight plastic or aluminum fenders, which keep gritty road water off you and your bike surprisingly well.

- Use wide, slightly underinflated tires to increase wet-road traction.

- Service your bike right after each wet ride. Hose it off, wipe it down with a towel, and then lubricate the chain and spray a water-dispersing product, such as WD-40, everywhere cables go into or out of housings. Give a spritz to the pivot points on brakes and derailleurs as well.

14. When buying or rebuilding wheels, get aluminum alloy spoke nipples. They're as reliable as conventional brass nipples and save a valuable ounce per wheel.

15. Carry a $10 bill and some quarters in your tire repair kit. You can buy snacks on long rides, phone home if you have a breakdown, or pay a driver to drop you off.

16. Just as your body needs to be outfitted for winter riding, so does your bike. Fenders (also known as mudguards) deflect slush that soaks clothing and fouls the drivetrain and brakes. Lightweight models are available for most bikes. Some snap onto the frame without the need for tools.

17. A rearview mirror is one of the most effective pieces of safety equipment a cyclist can use. It allows you to see what's behind without turning your head and shoulders, a potentially hazardous maneuver in traffic.

18. If the chuck of your floor pump blows off the valve stem when you reach higher pressures, position the wheel so you can hold the chuck with your foot. Better yet, buy a new chuck. Another solution is to cut a slot in the middle of a section of old inner tube. Make the hole just large enough for the chuck to squeeze through. Then place the chuck on the valve, and tie the ends of the tube around the tire. A similar trick can be done with a strip of hook-and-loop fastener.

19. Use grease, not oil, to lubricate the plunger's cupped washer inside a pump. Oil can get into the inner tube and rot the rubber.

20. To prevent a frame pump or a minipump from backfiring, place the head onto a presta valve just far enough to adequately grip it. Hold it steady in this position as you pump. It helps to loop your

(continued on page 128)

BUYING A NEW BIKE

If you're a serious enough cyclist to have read this far, you're probably ready to drop some serious coin on your new steed. Heck, it's not uncommon for avid cyclists to spend more on their bikes than they do on their cars (in fact, many consider it a matter of pride to do exactly that). If you're in the market for a new bike, this section is for you.

1. Find the right shop. Every good bike-buying experience begins with the right shop. How do you know if a shop is good? Ask around. The cycling community is tight-knit; word of mouth means more than flashy ads or promises.

2. Another sign of a good bike shop: They'll sponsor maintenance workshops and lead group rides for all ability levels.

3. Don't get hung up on brand. If you're shopping at a dedicated bike shop, you're going to find high-quality bicycles. That's not to say you shouldn't buy the bike of your dreams; only that there is effectively no quality difference between the major manufacturers.

4. Learn your frame materials. Not so long ago, high-end bicycles were built out of steel and steel only. Today there's aluminum, carbon fiber, steel, titanium, and practically every combination you can imagine. While building techniques play as large a part in ride quality as frame material, some generalities can be made.

   • Steel offers a smooth ride and relatively easy repairability but is typically heavier than more modern materials.

   • Aluminum is stiff, light, and inexpensive but won't last as long as steel, and transmits more road vibration to the rider.

   • Carbon fiber is light and can be easily "tuned" by the manufacturer to deliver desired ride qualities. It mutes road vibration but often feels slightly "dead." And it's usually expensive.

   • Titanium is light, offers a lively ride, and has a long fatigue life. Downsides? Expense, expense, and expense.

5. No matter what frame material you get on your new road bike, make sure it's equipped with a carbon fiber fork. Carbon forks eat road vibration for breakfast, lunch, and dinner while providing excellent steering qualities.

6. Most modern mountain bikes are constructed of aluminum. That's because suspension mitigates the abusive ride of the material. If you're shopping for an unsuspended "hardtail" mountain bike, look at easier-riding materials, such as steel, carbon fiber, or titanium.

7. Mountain bike suspension travel continues to grow. How much do you need? It depends on what you want to do with your new bike.

- If you're looking for a cross-country racer, choose a bike with 3 to 4 inches of travel.

- For general riding and occasional racing or for long-distance racing, look for a model that boasts 4 to 6 inches of travel front and rear.

- Aggressive riders and anyone looking to dip their tire treads in the freeriding waters should buy a bike with at least 6 and as many as 8 inches of travel.

8. The sweet spot of value and performance is at the $1,500 to $2,000 price point for road bikes and full-suspension mountain bikes. For unsuspended mountain bikes, it's $800 to $1,200.

9. Always budget at least $200 for riding gear. Unless you already have them, you're going to need a helmet, cycling shorts, and shoes, as well as a frame pump, saddle bag, and spare inner tube.

10. Ride, ride, ride. If the shop doesn't allow test rides, shop elsewhere. You should plan to spend many hours shopping for your new bike, and plan to spend most of these riding.

thumb over the tire. Accidentally pushing the head on too far will depress the valve, release the high pressure, and cause the pump handle to shoot back suddenly, possibly striking you and/or breaking the pump.

21. When shopping for a rechargeable lighting system, be aware that there are several types of batteries. The most common are lead acid, nickel cadmium (NiCad), and nickel metal hydride (NiMH). Lead acid batteries are less expensive, but they are heavier and they require more care. They should not be drained, which can damage them and reduce their life. Also, they can die for good if not used for a long time. NiCad and NiMH batteries, on the other hand, thrive on "deep cycling" (exhausting and recharging), so their life span is longer. However, they lose power rapidly at the end of their charge. You can go from bright to no light in just a few minutes.

22. Consider a helmet-mounted headlight if you ride on trails or roads that have lots of turns. Turning your head to look toward the inside of a corner fills the area with light. A helmet light also lets you track an object, and it's handy for making emergency repairs. Disadvantages include glare when riding in drizzle or fog, more weight on the head, and a chance that the helmet's protective qualities may be compromised in a crash.

23. If your floor pump is a few years old, be skeptical of what the built-in pressure gauge tells you. Old pumps may read low by as much as 20 psi. Underinflation causes greater rolling resistance and the risk of pinch flats.

24. To prevent your glasses from fogging, smear both sides of the lenses with a little gel toothpaste. Rinse with cold water; then dry with a towel.

25. If you intend to buy a hybrid bike (a cross between a road and a mountain bike), base its size on your intended use. If you're going to ride primarily on pavement, use your road bike size because crotch clearance isn't an issue. You don't need to dismount quickly and often, and the longer top tube will put you in a more efficient position. If you plan to use your hybrid for lots of off-road riding, too, choose a frame a couple of inches smaller than your road size, as you would for a mountain bike. You'll appreciate the extra crotch clearance during sudden dismounts. If you will be riding exclusively on dirt roads or off-road, consider a "comfort bike," essentially a mountain bike with suspension forks and seatpost and an upright riding position.

26. Silence annoying clicks and creaks in clipless pedals by applying a few drops of oil to each shoe's cleat where it contacts the sole and to the pedal-gripping hardware.

27. Coat your mountain bike's chain with a thick, gooey lubricant to protect it in muddy conditions. Coat your entire drivechain with a nonstick vegetable cooking spray.

28. Grease the quick-release and mounting bolt threads on your car rack to prevent them from seizing with corrosion.

29. Even the best lock won't save your bike unless it's used properly. Make your bike less of a target by locking it in a well-lit public area. Always secure the frame and the wheels, and examine the object you're locking them to. Ideally, it should be a metal post, such as a parking meter, with something at the top that prevents the bike from being lifted off. Thieves won't hesitate to steal your bike and lock, then separate them later.

30. U-locks are popular and effective, but they require a special technique. First, remove the front wheel and rest the frame's fork tips on the ground. Next, place the front wheel beside the rear wheel. The U encloses the two rims, seat tube, and post (or whatever you're locking to). Finally, the lock's crossbar is attached.

31. Whatever type of lock you use, don't place it near the ground. In this position, it's easier for a thief to apply leverage with tools or crush it with a hammer.

11

95 TIPS FOR BETTER BIKE CARE AND REPAIR

While it's true that modern bikes are marvels of technology, it's also true that most of the maintenance that keeps your bike running smoothly can be accomplished in your basement or garage with just a few tools and a modicum of mechanical sense. Bonus: When you understand how a bike works and take care of its basic needs yourself, you'll ride with more confidence and safety. Oh, and save money. Got your attention now?

1. The two easiest ways to help your bike work well are to keep the tires inflated to the recommended pressure listed on their sidewall, and keep the chain lubricated.

2. Don't procrastinate when it comes to bike maintenance. If you notice a problem, remedy it immediately after the ride. Otherwise, it may slip your mind till you're riding again.

3. Beware of using a gas station's air pump. It quickly delivers a large volume of air that can blow a bike tire off the rim. Invest in a good floor pump, as well as a frame or minipump.

4. Wrap a strip of tape around your bike's seatpost where it enters the frame. Then you can tell if the post slips and you can easily reset your saddle height if the post is removed.

5. Memorize the distance from the center of the crank axle to the top of the saddle, measured in line with the seatpost. It's good to know for when you need to ride a different bike for any reason.

6. Rotate your road tires. The rear tire wears more than twice as fast as the front, so switch them every 1,000 miles or so to get maximum life from each pair.

7. Carry a patch kit as well as a spare tube so you won't be stranded if you have two flats on a ride.

8. Carry two spare tubes on a rainy ride. Flats seem to occur more frequently on wet roads, and it's difficult to apply patches in damp conditions.

9. Check the glue in your patch kit periodically to be sure it hasn't evaporated.

10. The patches in most tube repair kits have foil on one side and clear plastic on the other. Carefully peel away the foil and place the patch against the tube after you've applied the glue. Leave the plastic on to prevent the patch from sticking to the inside of the tire.

11. Glueless patches make puncture repair quicker and simpler, but don't trust them to be a permanent fix. It's smart to replace a glueless patch with a conventional one when you're back home.

12. Use nylon-reinforced strapping tape as a protective rim strip. It's light and thin to aid tire installation and removal, and its adhesive prevents it from moving to uncover spoke heads. Cut the tape lengthwise, if necessary, so it fits precisely into the rim well.

13. Write your name, address, phone number, and "This bike was stolen" on a piece of masking tape and stick it to the fork's steerer tube. Then if the bike ever is ripped off, a shop mechanic may someday contact you in the midst of a repair and make your day.

14. Check tire inflation weekly if you're a recreational rider. Tubes may lose several pounds of pressure during this period. Under-inflated tires roll slower, wear faster, and increase the chances of pinch flats and rim damage.

15. Check tire inflation before each ride if you're a racer. When you train on the same tires, at the same pressure as those you race on, you become a better and more confident bike handler.

16. Align the tire label with the tube's valve stem during installation. This looks professional, and if you have a puncture, it gives you a reference point. You can easily match the hole in the tube to the tire to check for embedded material.

17. Silence annoying clicks and creaks in clipless pedals by applying silicone spray to the shoe's cleat where it contacts the sole, and to the pedal's cleat-gripping hardware. Wipe off any excess. Grit won't stick to silicone the way it will to an oily lube.

KEEP IT QUIET!

Sometimes a bike seems haunted by mysterious ticks, squeaks, and rattles. Here are their common hiding places and how to silence them.

1. When you hear a metallic click during every crank revolution, unscrew the pedals, grease their threads, and retighten them firmly.

2. A squeak is from a pedal rather than the chain if it occurs at the same place on each pedal stroke. For conventional pedals, spray lubrication on points where the cage and body connect. For clipless pedals, make sure all cleat contact points are clean. Apply a silicone spray to these points and wipe off the excess. Also make sure the cleats are tight. Spray silicone between each cleat and the sole.

3. If the chain chirps, it simply needs lubrication.

4. If the chain clicks or jumps, it has a tight link. To find it, kneel at the right side of the bike and turn the crank backward by hand. Watch the chain as it winds through the rear derailleur pulleys. An inflexible link will be apparent. Grasp the chain on either side of the stiff link (use rags to keep your hands clean), bend it laterally several times to loosen it, apply lubrication, and then recheck.

5. If the handlebar/stem creaks during sprints or climbs when lots of force is being applied, tighten the binder bolt (in front). If the

18. Keep handlebar ends plugged so they won't take a core sample from your body in a crash.

19. To keep out water and grit, place a small section of an old inner tube around a headset's lower bearing race the next time the headset is overhauled.

20. To confuse and perhaps foil a thief, adjust one brake so that when its quick-release is closed, it clamps the rim and prevents the wheel from rolling.

---

noise persists, loosen the binder bolt and spray a lubricant between the bar and stem; then retighten firmly.

6. Buzzing occurs when a bottle cage, frame pump, or some other add-on part is vibrating. Or it could be a cable housing vibrating against the frame. Touch these things while riding to isolate the problem; then tighten, shorten, reroute, or tape as necessary.

7. Rattles and jingles can come from a seat bag (wrap metal items with rubber bands or rags; put coins in a change purse). They could be caused by a loose dustcap on a hub, a loose bottom bracket lockring, or loose cassette cogs. Remedy these problems right away, or the next sound you hear could be the cash register after an expensive repair.

8. Thumping is usually felt rather than heard. Common causes are dented rims and bulging or improperly seated tires.

9. Clicking during out-of-saddle climbing or sprinting sometimes comes from two spokes rubbing together. Put a drop of oil on each spoke crossing.

10. Noises are transmitted quite efficiently by frame tubes, especially aluminum ones. You might swear a creak or click is coming from your cranks or bottom bracket, but it could easily be your saddle rails, handlebar/stem interface, or quick release skewer/dropout.

21. If your mountain bike has a quick-release seatpost, remove it and secure it with your lock (or take it with you) when leaving the bike unattended.

22. Hose down your bike while it's still wet from a rainy ride; then dry it with a towel. Lube the chain and the pivot points of the derailleurs and brakes. Spray a water-dispersing product, such as WD-40, into places where cables enter or exit housings.

23. Carry a tire "boot" in your patch kit to repair large cuts or sidewall damage. This could be a piece of clincher tire or canvas. Place it under the cut, between the tire and tube.

24. That old standby, duct tape, can come in handy. For example, it can be used like a boot to line the inside of a torn tire. Keep some wrapped around a tire lever in your seat bag.

25. Wrap handlebar tape by starting from each end and working toward the stem. Then your hands will push with the overlaps, not against them, and the tape won't separate. Secure the ends near the stem with black or colored plastic tape.

26. If you frequently bend or break hub axles, have the alignment of your frame's dropouts checked.

27. If you're using tubular (sew-up) tires and change one on the road because of a flat, help the spare bond to the rim by heating the glue. Do this by riding for a few minutes with the brake lightly applied.

28. For a special, relatively short event such as a time trial, remove the grease from your hub bearings and replace it with light oil. This reduces friction to the minimum. Oil quickly leaks out, though, so don't continue to use the wheels before repacking the hubs with grease.

29. Don't use a narrow tire on a wide rim. It reduces protection, increasing the risk of your damaging the rim when riding over potholes or rocks.

30. Check all nuts and bolts on a new bike after the first week of use.

If anything is going to loosen, it'll usually happen during the initial miles.

31. Apply a bike wax to preserve the frame's finish and make it easier to clean, but keep wax away from brakes and rims.

32. Always take a new bike back for the free 30-day checkup that most shops offer. (Mark the date on your calendar.) The mechanics are trained to spot slight problems that you may not even notice but that can eventually damage parts or cause a breakdown if not corrected.

33. After installing a clincher tire, be sure it's properly seated. Do this by spinning the wheel and watching the bead (the thin line molded into the rubber just above the rim). The bead should be steady all the way around on both sides. If it bobs up or dips below the rim, deflate the tire and massage the area to work the tire and tube into place; then inflate again. Sometimes a low bead won't pop into place until higher pressures are reached.

34. If there are wobbles in the line between a tire's tan sidewall and black tread, don't worry about it as long as the bead line is correct. Most tires have some irregularity in the tread line. It doesn't affect performance.

35. If you have Schrader valves and one tire loses air more rapidly than the other, its valve may be loose. Check this by inflating the tire to full pressure and putting saliva across the valve opening. A slowly forming bubble tells you the core needs to be tightened. It takes a special little tool, so drop by a bike shop or garage to see if a mechanic will do it for you for free.

36. If you can't get factory touch-up paint for your bike's color, check a toy store for the model enamel that's closest to being right. You can even mix colors to arrive at an exact match.

37. Monitor wear on a treadless road tire by checking the width of the section that contacts the road. As the tire wears, this section becomes wider.

38. Replace a tire if the fabriclike casing material appears through the tread. Bulges, cracks, or cuts in the sidewall are also grounds for replacement.

39. A quick-release wheel is tight enough in the frame if closing the lever leaves an imprint on your palm.

40. To check headset adjustment, stand beside the bike, squeeze the front brake lever, and rock the bike back and forth. A loose headset will be apparent. If it seems okay, check for tightness by slightly lifting the front of the bike and letting the handlebar turn from one extreme to the other. If it sticks in either direction, the headset is tight and should be adjusted or overhauled.

41. To bring a worn, pitted headset back to life, toss out the bottom race's bearing retainer and install loose balls. Without the retainer, the race can hold at least one additional bearing. They can't settle into all the same dents, so the headset won't feel nearly as rough.

42. Hang your bike by the wheels if that's the easiest way for you to store it. Hanging won't cause damage. In fact, it stresses wheels less than riding on them.

43. Periodically inspect each tire's tread for embedded glass, thorns, and other debris. Use a flashlight to get a good look. You can often prevent punctures by removing sharp things before they work through to the tube.

44. Don't discard an entire $60 cassette just because one or two $7 cogs are excessively worn. In fact, a good-quality cassette hub is capable of outlasting several generations of cogs. On the other hand, if most of the cogs are significantly worn (thin, hooked teeth), it's smarter to replace them all than to mix several new ones with the old ones. If the worn cogs are among the three or four largest, you will have to replace the whole cassette because these cogs are riveted in to place.

45. To stop high-speed front-end shimmy, accelerate, decelerate, or

POSTCRASH CHECKLIST ►►►►

After a crash, it can be hard to spot the damage your bike has suffered. Here's a quick checklist that covers all the major parts. If you suspect a problem, take the bike to a shop mechanic for a more extensive evaluation and repairs. Don't risk your safety by riding a damaged bike.

1. **Frame.** Inspect all tube intersections for wrinkles, bulges, and cracks in the paint. These are signs of a bent frame.

2. **Fork.** A straightedge held beside the fork should bisect the head tube of the frame and the fork's top section (unless it's a fork with straight rather than curved blades). Also, an undamaged wheel should sit perfectly centered between the blades. If it's closer to one blade than the other, the fork has been bent.

3. **Wheels.** Spin each one and look for lateral or vertical movement at the rim. Minor hops and wobbles can be removed by truing. Big wavers may mean broken spokes or a bent rim, conditions that require professional service.

4. **Other parts.** Look for scratches, dents, and bends on every component. Pedals and brake levers can take a beating in a crash. The rear derailleur is susceptible to damage even if the bike merely falls over on its right side. Kneel behind to see if its cage hangs parallel to the cogs. If it's bent inward, don't ride until it's been realigned. A shift could put the cage into the spokes, causing mayhem.

lean hard on the handlebar. It also helps to clamp the top tube between your knees. The reasons shimmy occurs aren't clearly understood or the same in every case. Suspected contributors are a short wheelbase, light wheels, an out-of-true front wheel, a loose front axle, a pitted or loose headset, a flexible frame, long tubes (large frame size), a bent fork, a misaligned frame, and a riding position that puts insufficient weight on the front wheel.

46. Don't base your service schedule for hubs on mileage or time. Rather, remove the wheels from your bike monthly (twice a month for mountain bikes ridden hard off-road), and spin each axle between your thumb and forefinger. When hub cones are properly adjusted, the axle will turn smoothly without grinding or binding. But if it turns without any resistance at all, it means the grease has washed out or dried up. It's time to repack the bearings.

47. The axle of a properly adjusted hub should have a hint of looseness to allow for compression when the wheel is tightened into the frame.

48. When fixing a flat, don't install the new tube before carefully feeling around the inside circumference of the tire. Whatever caused the puncture may still be stuck through the tread, ready to strike again. Pick it out with your fingernail, a pocketknife, or the corner of a small screwdriver.

49. If a spoke breaks, stop right away. Remove it by unscrewing it from the nipple, or twist it around a neighbor. Especially in the rear wheel, a flapping spoke can snag something (the derailleur, for instance) and cause major damage.

50. Prevent snakebites! Not only the reptilian kind, but those two tiny punctures caused by the tube's being pinched against the rim flange when you ride over a rock or other abrupt obstacle. An underinflated tire is more likely to bottom out like this, but rider weight is another factor. If you're heavy, use wider tires and be sure they're inflated to the maximum pressure listed on the sidewall. It also helps to slow down for obstacles and reduce the weight on each wheel as it makes contact.

51. When the location of a puncture can be easily identified, save both time and your spare tube by making the repair this way: Pry about 6 inches of bead from the rim on either side of the hole, and pull out only as much tube as necessary to patch it. Then simply reinsert the tube, reseat the bead, and inflate.

52. When taking your bike on a plane, play it safe and reduce tire pressure to about half of normal. Even though baggage compartments are pressurized, this will prevent a blowout in case the level varies, yet it leaves sufficient air to protect the rims during handling.

53. If your bike has a steel frame and you live in a damp climate, undercoat the inside of the tubes to prevent rust. A product made specifically for this is called J. P. Weigle's Frame Saver, available at bike shops.

54. If you ride much in inclement weather, install fenders. They keep lots of grit off your bike, reducing cleanup time and maintenance. Your components will last longer, too. Use full-size fenders—the more of the wheels they cover, the better.

55. Rub paraffin wax on the derailleur cables where they pass under the bottom bracket, after you loosen and clean them. Paraffin provides lubrication so the cables slide smoothly, but grit won't stick to it like it does to grease or oil.

56. Pinch the tires every time you get off your bike during a ride, just to be sure there isn't a slow-leaking puncture.

57. Whenever possible, lubricate your chain 24 hours before the next ride. This time gap allows the lube's liquid carrier to evaporate. The drivetrain will stay cleaner because less grit will stick to the chain, and less lube will be flung onto the frame and rear wheel. It helps to let the lube sit overnight, and then wipe off the excess before riding.

58. If the chain becomes dry or its rollers look shiny, you've waited too long to lubricate. The exception is when using a so-called dry lube, which is designed to evaporate completely.

59. Turn barrel adjusters counterclockwise to remove slack from cables without tools. These adjusters are found where cables connect to the rear derailleur and to most brakes or brake levers. On some bikes they're also found on the down-tube cable guides.

60. Here are two easy, no-tool ways to remedy poor rear shifting.

- If the chain balks at climbing to bigger cogs, turn the rear derailleur's barrel adjuster counterclockwise half a turn (see photo). Check performance and continue with half turns until shifts are smooth and quick.

- If the chain is slow to shift to smaller cogs, use the same procedure, but turn the barrel adjuster clockwise. If you have one of Shimano's Rapid-Rise derailleurs, reverse the above procedure.

61. To fix a cut tire in an emergency, fashion a boot from handlebar tape, an energy bar wrapper, or roadside litter. A piece of a coated paper drinking cup works well. So does a folded dollar bill because it's made of relatively tough linen, not plain paper.

62. Armor All and similar products help keep rubber brake lever hoods from drying and cracking. Don't use it on tires, though. It makes them slippery and can get on the rims, hindering braking.

63. Hot or cold weather won't harm a bike, but avoid subjecting it to extreme differences in temperature or humidity. For instance, if you move your bike from a cold garage to a heated house, the temperature change will cause condensation inside the tubes and components. The same thing will happen when you take it from an air-conditioned house into warm, humid air. This condensation is especially bad for steel frames because it can cause rust.

64. Buy your bike grease in small tubes or containers. A large jar of grease is more likely to become contaminated by dirt as you continually dip into it. Also, it's neater to squeeze grease into a bearing race from a tube than to smear it in with a finger.

65. For best results, use two types of grease: a smooth, light version for cassette bearings and semisealed components (where an O-ring helps keep the grease in place), and a tackier, thicker version for pedals, nonsealed bearings, headsets, and bottom brackets where the grease is likely to ooze out and a moisture barrier is needed.

66. Presta valves often stick closed even though you've unscrewed their little metal cap. You pump, but no air enters. The solution is simple. Before attaching the pump, depress the valve fully to release a shot of air. Then the pump can work.

67. Adjust your road bike's tire pressure to meet special riding needs. For instance, shock absorption and cornering traction are improved by running several pounds less than the recommended maximum pressure. The resulting increase in comfort and road holding will be appreciated on long rides or when you're riding in the rain. Conversely, adding several pounds more than the stated maximum decreases rolling resistance. This helps in a road race or time trial, where comfort and cornering are less important than speed.

68. The maximum inflation imprinted on a clincher sidewall leaves plenty of fudge factor. In most cases, manufacturers build their tires to withstand up to twice the recommended pressure.

69. Once each month, inspect your rims for cracks and your tires for casing damage. The best way to see these things is to overinflate the tires by 15 psi or so. The increased stress will make any problems more visible. Use a bright light for a good look, and remember to bleed off the extra air before you ride.

70. If you don't have a dishing gauge to determine whether the rim of a wheel is centered on the hub, use your bike frame. Simply flip the wheel over and see if the rim is in the same position relative to the brake pads.

(continued on page 144)

KEEP YOUR MOUNTAIN BIKE ROLLIN' SMOOTH

Modern mountain bikes drip with complicated technology. They're almost ubiquitously equipped with front suspension forks, and rear suspension is now the norm rather than the exception. Stopping power often comes courtesy of hydraulic disc brakes, drivetrains now boast as many as 27 gears (3 in front; 9 out back), and tubeless tires have gained widespread appeal. Keep it all rolling smoothly with these tips.

1. Examine your shocks—front and rear—weekly for evidence of oil leaks. A thin film of oil residue is normal, but drips and puddles are not. If you find them, visit your shop ASAP.

2. To get the most out of your suspension, it should "bottom out" (use all of its travel) at least once each ride. Attach a zip tie to the inner fork legs so you can see how much travel you are using. You can do the same with the rear shock.

3. Don't be afraid to adjust your suspension settings. Modern shocks are incredibly responsive to even minute adjustments, and the improvement in ride quality can be astounding. Here are some general guidelines.

- If your suspension is too soft or blows through its travel too quickly, increase the compression damping and preload adjustments. If you're larger than average or you simply ride more aggressively than most, you may need to have your local shop install heavier shock oil.

- Likewise, if your suspension is too firm, decrease compression damping and preload and consider a lighter-weight oil.

- If your suspension "packs up" and doesn't seem to return to its fully suspended state during sections of trail that feature frequent bumps, decrease rebound damping, which will help it spring back from bumps more quickly.

- If it feels like your suspension bounces back too quickly, increase rebound damping. This will slow its return.

4. When hydraulic disc brakes feel mushy, it's because they are low on fluid and need to be bled. Although you can do this at home, it's a job best left to a qualified mechanic.

5. Get in the habit of checking your disc brake pads. Because they're not as easy to see as rim brake pads, it's easy to forget about them. To check them, remove the wheel and look inside the brake with a flashlight.

6. Never pull on a hydraulic disc brake lever when the wheel is not installed. Without the brake rotor to press against, the pads won't be able to retract properly.

7. It is normal for the rotor to rub against the brake pads lightly when you spin the wheel without the brake applied. But if it catches suddenly or makes lots of noise, suspect a bent disc rotor.

8. Contrary to popular belief, tubeless tires do *not* eliminate pinch flats. Although you can get away with slightly lower tire pressures for increased traction and comfort, don't drop your normal pressure by more than 20 percent, or you risk damaging the sidewalls of your tubeless tires.

9. Even with tubeless, you should carry a spare tube. That's because tubeless tires will accept a tube, and it's far quicker to fix a flat on the trail in this manner, rather than a time-consuming tire patch.

10. If possible, install tubeless tires with an air compressor. The quick blast of air makes it much easier to seat the tire bead.

11. Because of the tight spacing necessary to fit nine cogs where we once had eight, modern drivetrains are more prone to clogging by mud, leaves, and grass. Be aware of this, and clean them regularly.

12. If you're a maintainance-phobe, consider cable-activated disc brakes. The best models, like those from Avid, offer nearly as much stopping power as hydraulics and are far easier to adjust.

13. Even the best shocks eventually develop play, and need to be rebuilt. You'll know this is the case with yours if the rear wheel can be moved from side to side (check your hub to be sure the movement isn't coming from there) or if you feel movement in the front end when you apply the front brake and rock the bike back and forth (again, this type of play can come from the headset, so be sure that's properly adjusted before digging into your suspension fork).

14. The more pivots a suspension frame has, the more chances for failure. Keep that in mind when shopping.

71. Put your patch kit, tire levers, and other tools in an old sock before storing them in your seat bag. This keeps everything organized and quiet. When you need to make a repair, pull the sock over your hand if you need to touch greasy parts.

72. Here's a trick for improving the rolling efficiency of a low- to medium-quality hub or bottom bracket. First, disassemble the component and wipe all parts clean. Then rebuild it, using the old bearings and a mildly abrasive metal polishing paste (such as Simichrome), instead of grease. Ride the bike about 5 miles so the paste will burnish the cones and races. Thoroughly clean the parts and repack them with grease and new, high-quality bearings.

73. To gauge the wear on a chain, hold a tape measure to the lower section between the rear derailleur and crankset. Put the tape's first mark on the center of any rivet; then look at the 12-inch mark. On a new chain it, too, will be on the center of a rivet. If the 12-inch mark falls ⅛ inch or more short of a rivet, the chain is worn (stretched) and should be replaced.

74. Whenever you replace a chain, take a test ride to check for skipping. Pedal in each cog, gingerly at first; then gradually increase the force. Stay seated in case what you're looking for actually happens. Excessively worn cogs will not mate with a new chain, so replace the ones that skip. If most do, it will probably be cheaper to replace the entire cluster. The best way to prolong the life of your drivetrain is to replace your chain often.

75. When using a chain tool to remove a non-Shimano chain for cleaning, don't drive the rivet completely out because it's very difficult to reinstall. Don't even push the rivet so far through that the chain falls apart on its own. Stop when the rivet is flush with the tool's back edge; then flex the chain sideways to snap it apart. (For a Shimano chain, drive the rivet all the way out, and then use the company's special replacement rivet to rejoin it.) SRAM chains have a special connecter link that allows you to break the chain without tools.

76. Don't have a special replacement rivet for your Shimano chain? If you're careful, you can separate the chain and rejoin it with a regular rivet, using the standard procedure described in tip 75.

77. Never use gas to clean your chain or other drivetrain components. It's not only flammable but will strip the parts of all lubrication. Instead, use kerosene or diesel fuel, both of which clean well but leave a light, oily film. Or use a citrus-based solvent.

78. Discard a chain that has several tight links or rust.

79. Don't be concerned about the frame flex you see when pedaling on an indoor trainer. Frames are resilient and designed to bend under load. When a bike is immobilized in a trainer, the flex is more apparent than it is on a road or trail. It's happening outside, too, but the bike is free to pivot on the tires.

80. A wobbly chainring can be trued with an adjustable wrench. Open the jaw just wide enough to slip it onto the ring at the wobble; then carefully pry inward or outward as necessary. Go easy and keep spinning the crank to check progress. Use the front derailleur's cage as a guide.

81. If noises or wobbles in the bike's rear hub make you suspect that the axle is broken, do not remove the wheel until you get back home. The quick-release skewer will hold the axle together.

82. If a wheel goes out of true, squeeze pairs of spokes to determine if one or more have loosened. If so, simply making them as tight as their same-side neighbors should eliminate the wobbles.

83. There's no danger in keeping your bike mounted on an indoor trainer. The rear tire might develop a flat spot where it rests against the roller, but this will quickly disappear when you pedal.

84. Scraping noises from the crank area probably mean the chain is rubbing the front derailleur. This happens as shifts with the rear derailleur alter the angle of the chain through the front cage.

Adjust the limit screws and/or cable tension on your front derailleur so that the shift detents center the cage around the chain.

85. Clatter from the rear of the bike after a shift means the chain isn't lined up directly with the cog it's on. It could be touching the next larger cog or angled toward the next-smaller one. Assuming the derailleur hasn't been bent or twisted by a crash, you can eliminate the rattling by turning its cable adjuster barrel (clockwise if the chain is touching a larger cog). Sight from behind until the chain drops straight to the derailleur.

86. Extreme chain angles—such as when you're combining the largest rear cog with the large chainring (or smallest cog with the small chainring)—may never run quietly or smoothly, which is one reason to avoid them. Another is excessive wear to chainring teeth. This is particularly a problem with mountain bikes, with their triple chainrings and huge rear cogs.

87. When setting up a bike repair area in your basement or garage, don't use a pegboard and hooks for hanging your tools. A pegboard requires mounting hardware and limits your choices for tool arrangement. Instead, get a 4-by-8-foot sheet of ¾-inch plywood. Use a large piece of cardboard as a template. Lay it down and trace the outline of your tools on it, arranging the most frequently used ones in the center. Place this template on the board, and drive finish nails into the outlines in positions that will support the tools. Remove the template and hang the tools. Trace their outline on the board with a black marker so you'll know where everything goes.

88. To make a holder for screwdrivers and Allen wrenches, drill vertical holes through a short 2-by-4-inch piece of wood. Attach it to your tool board and drop the tools through.

89. Use a stain-resistant indoor/outdoor carpet for your home shop area. It should be a solid light color. This makes it easy to find small parts if you drop them. Avoid mottled patterns, shaggy textures, and wood floors with cracks.

90. If the chain skips and slips in a certain gear, the problem is a worn cog. If it happens in all gears, the problem is a stiff link.

91. To solve a disconcerting creak that occurs when climbing in the saddle, apply spray lube where the seat rails contact the seatpost clamp and where the rails enter the seat's plastic shell.

92. Short Allen keys and poor-fitting wrenches can prevent you from tightening or adjusting parts properly. But oversize wrenches can cause overtightening and damage. Always use small tools on small nuts and bolts, particularly when you work with carbon fiber components, which are highly susceptible to damage when overtightened. If more leverage is required on an Allen key, slip an adjustable wrench or a small pipe over its end.

93. Some riders carry CO_2 inflation cartridges in lieu of a minipump. These devices are light, fast, and efficient. Practice with one before relying on it, though. If improperly applied, it will just freeze your valve stem and leave your tire flat.

94. Make sure your brake pads match your rims. Ceramic-coated or carbon rims require special brake pads.

95. Removing handlebar grips on a mountain bike is easy if you slide a small flat-bladed screwdriver under the grip and spray some WD-40 in the gap.

Anatomy of a Bike

saddle rails
*(saddle can be slid forward
or backward along these)*

saddle

seatpost
*(holds saddle and
determines its tilt)*

seatpost binder
*(a quick-release here allows
saddle to be raised
or lowered without tools)*

seat tube
(length determines frame size)

rear brake

seatstay

freewheel or cassette
*(collection of five to nine cogs
of varied number of teeth)*

chainstay

chain

rear dropout
*(slots in which rear
hub axle fits)*

cable housing
(routes and protects wire cable)

derailleur adjustment barrel
*(allows fine-tuning of cable
length; similar mechanism
may be found on brakes)*

rear derailleur
*(moves chain from cog to cog;
controlled by right shift lever)*

derailleur pulleys
(direct chain through rear derailleur)

cable stop
*(anchors the housing for
the cable to pull against)*

front derailleur
*(moves chain from chainring
to chainring; controlled by
left shift lever)*

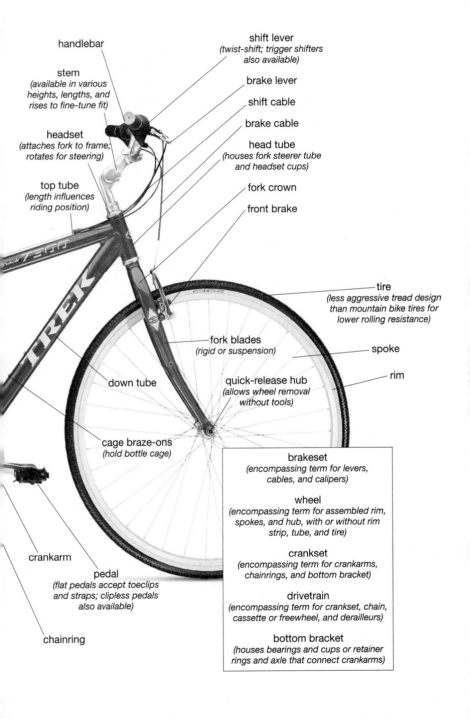

handlebar

stem
*(available in various
heights, lengths, and
rises to fine-tune fit)*

headset
*(attaches fork to frame;
rotates for steering)*

top tube
*(length influences
riding position)*

shift lever
*(twist-shift; trigger shifters
also available)*

brake lever

shift cable

brake cable

head tube
*(houses fork steerer tube
and headset cups)*

fork crown

front brake

tire
*(less aggressive tread design
than mountain bike tires for
lower rolling resistance)*

fork blades
(rigid or suspension)

spoke

down tube

rim

quick-release hub
*(allows wheel removal
without tools)*

cage braze-ons
(hold bottle cage)

crankarm

pedal
*(flat pedals accept toeclips
and straps; clipless pedals
also available)*

chainring

brakeset
*(encompassing term for levers,
cables, and calipers)*

wheel
*(encompassing term for assembled rim,
spokes, and hub, with or without rim
strip, tube, and tire)*

crankset
*(encompassing term for crankarms,
chainrings, and bottom bracket)*

drivetrain
*(encompassing term for crankset, chain,
cassette or freewheel, and derailleurs)*

bottom bracket
*(houses bearings and cups or retainer
rings and axle that connect crankarms)*

GLOSSARY

One final tip: Learn the lingo. This glossary will help you understand cycling's many special words and phrases when you're visiting bike shops or chatting with other riders. Though not every term is used in this book, you'll hear them all when you're involved in the sport.

A

Aerobic: Exercise at an intensity that allows the body's need for oxygen to be continually met. This level of intensity can be sustained for long periods.

Aerodynamic: A design of cycling equipment or a riding position that reduces wind resistance. "Aero" for short.

Anaerobic: Exercise above the intensity at which the body's need for oxygen can be met. This intensity can be sustained only briefly.

Apex: The sharpest part of a turn where the transition from entering to exiting takes place.

Attack: An aggressive, high-speed jump away from other riders.

B

Balaclava: A thin hood that covers the head and neck with an opening for the face. It's worn under the helmet to prevent heat loss in cold or wet conditions.

Bead: In tires, the edge along each side's inner circumference that fits into the rim.

Berm: Small embankment along the edge of a trail, often occurring in turns.

Block: To legally impede the progress of opposing riders to allow team-mates a better chance of success.

Blood glucose: A sugar, glucose is the only fuel that can be used by the brain.

Blow up: To suddenly be unable to continue at the required pace, due to overexertion.

Bonk: A state of severe exhaustion caused mainly by the depletion of glycogen in the muscles because the rider has failed to eat or drink enough. Once it occurs, rest and high-carbohydrate foods are necessary for recovery.

Boot: A small piece of material used inside a tire to cover a cut in the tread or sidewall. Without it, the tube will push through and blow out.

Bottom bracket: The part of the frame where the crankset is installed. Also, the axle, cups, and bearings of the crankset.

BPM: Abbreviation for beats per minute, in reference to heart rate.

Break, breakaway: A rider or group of riders that has escaped the pack.

Bridge, bridge a gap: To catch a rider or group that has opened a lead.

Bunch: The main cluster of riders in a race. Also called the group, pack, field, or peloton.

Bunnyhop: A way to ride over obstacles such as rocks or logs in which both wheels leave the ground.

C

Cadence: The number of times during 1 minute that a pedal stroke is com-pleted. Also called pedal rpm.

Carbohydrate: In the diet, it is broken down to glucose, the body's prin-cipal energy source, through digestion and metabolism. It is stored as glycogen in the liver and muscles. Carbo can be simple (sugars) or complex (bread, pasta, grains, fruits, vegetables). Complex carbohydrates contain additional nutrients. One gram of carbohydrate supplies 4 calories.

Cardiovascular: Pertaining to the heart and blood vessels.

Cassette: The set of gear cogs on the rear hub. Also called a cogset, cluster, or block.

Catch air: When both wheels leave the ground, usually because of a rise or dip in the riding surface.

Categories: The division of racers based on ability and/or experience. "Cat" for short. In road racing, cat 1 through 5. In mountain biking, pro, expert, sport, and beginner.

Century: A 100-mile ride. A 62-mile ride is known as a metric century.

Chainring: A sprocket on the crankset. There may be one, two, or three. Short version is ring.

Chainsuck: When the chain sticks to the chainring teeth during a downshift and gets drawn up and jammed between the small ring and the frame. Particularly a problem in a mountain bike's granny ring (*see* Granny ring).

Chasers: Those who are trying to catch a group or a lead rider.

Chondromalacia: A serious knee injury in which there is disintegration of cartilage surfaces due to improper tracking of the kneecap. Symptoms start with deep knee pain and a crunching sensation during bending.

Circuit: A course that is ridden two or more times to compose the race.

Circuit training: A weight training technique in which you move rapidly from exercise to exercise without rest.

Clean: In mountain biking, to ride through a difficult, technical section without putting a foot down.

Cleat: A metal or plastic fitting on the sole of a cycling shoe that engages the pedal.

Clincher: A conventional tire with a separate inner tube.

Clydesdale: A large rider. At some mountain bike races, there is a Clydesdale class for riders who weigh more than 200 pounds.

Cog: A sprocket on the rear wheel's cassette.

Compression damping: How you control a shock's response to bumps.

Contact patch: The portion of a tire in touch with the ground.

Crash rash: Any skin abrasion resulting from a fall. Also called road rash.

Criterium: A mass-start race covering numerous laps of a course that is normally about 1 mile or less in length. "Crit" for short.

Cross-country: The traditional and most popular type of mountain bike race. Most courses mix fire roads (where you can pass or be passed) with singletrack (where passing is difficult). Races may be point to point, one long loop, or two or more laps of a shorter loop.

Cross training: Combining sports for mental refreshment and physical conditioning, especially during cycling's off-season.

Cyclocross: A fall or winter event contested mostly or entirely off pavement. Courses include obstacles, steps, and steep hills that force riders to dismount and run with their bikes.

D

Dab: To put a foot on the ground to prevent falling over.

Doubletrack: Two parallel trails formed by the wheel ruts of off-road vehicles. Also called a Jeep trail.

Downhill: A race held at ski areas. The fastest rider from top to bottom wins. Competitors wear protective clothes and pads (body armor) and usually ride special dual-suspension bikes designed for maximum shock absorption.

Downshift: To shift to a lower gear—that is, a larger cog or a smaller chainring.

Draft: To ride closely behind another rider to take advantage of the windbreak (slipstream), which uses about 20 percent less energy. Also called sitting in or wheelsucking.

Drivetrain: The components directly involved with making the rear wheel turn. Comprised of the chain, crankset, cassette or freewheel, and derailleurs. Also called the power train.

Drop: A maneuver in mountain biking in which the bike is jumped down off a terrain feature while remaining horizontal.

Drops: The lower part of a down-turned handlebar typically found on a road bike. The curved portions are called the hooks.

Dualie: A bike with front and rear suspension. Short for dual suspension.

Dual slalom: As with skiing, riders race downhill between gates on parallel courses. Unlike in a downhill race, in which the clock determines the winner, dual slalom is head-to-head elimination. Riders continue advancing until they lose.

E

Echelon: A form of paceline in which the riders angle off behind one another to get maximum draft in a crosswind.

Elastomer: A compressible, rubberlike material used to absorb shock in some suspension systems.

Electrolyte: Substance—such as sodium, potassium, or chloride—that is necessary for muscle contraction and maintenance of fluid levels.

Endo: To crash by going over the bike's handlebar. Short for end over end.

Ergometer: A stationary, bicycle-like device with adjustable pedal resistance used in physiological testing or indoor training.

F

Fartlek: A Swedish word meaning *speed play*, it is a training technique based on unstructured changes in pace and intensity. It can be used instead of timed or measured intervals.

Fat: In the diet, the most concentrated source of food energy, supplying 9 calories per gram. Stored fat provides about half the energy required for low-intensity exercise.

Feed zone: A designated area on a racecourse where riders can be handed food and drinks.

Field sprint: The dash for the finish line by the main group of riders.

Fire road: A dirt or gravel road in the backcountry wide enough to allow access by emergency vehicles.

Fixed gear: A direct-drive setup using one chainring and one rear cog, as on a track bike. When the rear wheel turns, so do the chain and crank; coasting isn't possible.

Freeride: A style of mountain biking involving elements of observed trials and downhilling, usually done on fully suspended frames.

Full suspension: A mountain bike having both a suspension fork and a suspension rear triangle.

Full tuck: An extremely crouched position used for maximum speed on descents.

G

General classification: The overall standings in a stage race. Often referred to as GC.

Glutes: The gluteal muscles of the buttocks. They are key to pedaling power.

Glycogen: A fuel derived as glucose (sugar) from carbohydrate and stored in the muscles and liver. It's the primary energy source for high-intensity cycling. Reserves are normally depleted after about 2½ hours of riding.

Glycogen window: The period within an hour after exercise when depleted muscles are most receptive to restoring their glycogen content. Eating foods or drinking fluids rich in carbohydrate enhances energy stores and recovery.

Gorp: Good ol' raisins and peanuts, a high-energy mix for nibbling during rides. Can also include nuts, seeds, M & M's, or granola.

Granny gear: The lowest gear ratio, combining the small chainring with the largest cassette cog. It's mainly used for very steep climbs. Named after the gear that grandmothers use most frequently.

Granny ring: The smallest of the three chainrings on a triple crankset.

H

Hammer: To ride strongly in big gears.

Hamstrings: The muscles on the backs of the thighs; not well-developed by cycling.

Hang in: To barely maintain contact at the back of the pack.

Hardtail: A mountain bike with no rear suspension.

Headset: The parts at the top and bottom of the frame's head tube into which the handlebar stem and fork are fitted.

Hybrid: A bike that combines features of road and mountain bikes. Also called a cross bike.

I

IMBA: International Mountain Bicycling Association, an organization dedicated to protecting and expanding trail access for mountain bikers.

Intervals: A structured method of training that alternates brief, hard efforts with short periods of easier riding for partial recovery.

J

Jam: A period of hard, fast riding.

Jump: A quick, hard acceleration.

L

Lactate threshold (LT): The exertion level beyond which the body can no longer produce energy aerobically, resulting in the buildup of lactic acid. This is marked by muscle fatigue, pain, and shallow, rapid breathing. Also called anaerobic threshold (AT).

Lactic acid: A substance formed during anaerobic metabolism when there is incomplete breakdown of glucose. It rapidly produces muscle fatigue and pain. Also called lactate.

Leadout: A race tactic in which a rider accelerates to his maximum speed for the benefit of a teammate in tow. The second rider then leaves the draft and sprints past at even greater speed near the finish line.

LSD: Long, steady distance, a training technique that requires a firm aerobic pace for at least 2 hours.

M

Mass start: Events such as road races, cross-country races, and criteriums in which all contestants leave the starting line at the same time.

Max VO₂: The maximum amount of oxygen that can be consumed during all-out exertion. This is a key indicator of a person's potential in cycling and other aerobic sports. It's largely genetically determined but can be improved somewhat by training.

Metric century: A 100-kilometer ride (62 miles).

Minuteman: In a time trial, the rider who is one place in front of you in the starting order. So called because in most TTs, riders start on 1-minute intervals.

Motorpace: To ride behind a motorcycle or other vehicle that breaks the wind.

Mudguard: Fender.

N

NORBA: National Off-Road Bicycling Association, the governing body of off-road racing in America. A division of USA Cycling.

O

Observed trials: A slow-speed event in which the objective is to ride a difficult, obstacle-filled course without putting a foot down. The rider with the fewest dabs wins. Also called simply trials.

Off the back: Describes one or more riders who have failed to keep pace with the main group. Also referred to as OTB.

Orthotic: Custom-made support worn in shoes to help neutralize biomechanical imbalances in the feet or legs.

Overgear: Using a gear ratio too big for the terrain or level of fitness.

Overtraining: Deep-seated fatigue, both physical and mental, caused by training at an intensity or volume too great for adaptation.

Oxygen debt: The amount of oxygen that must be consumed to pay back the deficit incurred by anaerobic work.

P

Paceline: A group formation in which each rider takes a turn breaking the wind at the front before pulling off, dropping to the rear position, and riding the others' draft until at the front once again.

Pannier: A large bike bag used by touring cyclists or commuters. Panniers attach to racks that place them low on each side of the rear wheel, and sometimes the front wheel.

Peak: A relatively short period during which maximum performance is achieved.

Peloton: A French word meaning the main group of riders in a race.

Periodization: The process of dividing training into specific phases by weeks or months.

Pinch flat: An internal puncture marked by two small holes caused by the tube's being squeezed against the rim. It results from riding into an object too hard for the air pressure in the tube. Also called a snakebite.

Portage: To lift and carry the bike, as when crossing a stream, a ditch, or ground too rocky to ride.

Power: The combination of speed and strength.

Preload: The adjustable spring tension in a suspension fork or rear shock. It determines how far the suspension compresses under body weight and how much travel remains to absorb impacts.

Presta: The narrow, European-style valve found on some inner tubes. A small metal cap on its end must be unscrewed before air can enter or exit.

Prime: A special award given to the leader on selected laps during a criterium or the first rider to reach a certain landmark in a road or cross-country race. It's used to heighten the action. Pronounced "preem."

Protein: In the diet, a substance required for tissue growth and repair. Composed of structural units called amino acids, protein is not a significant energy source unless not enough calories and carbohydrate are consumed. One gram of protein equals 4 calories.

PSI: Abbreviation for pounds per square inch. The unit of measure for tire inflation and air pressure in some suspensions.

Pull; pull through: To take a turn at the front of a pack of riders.

Pull off: To move to the side after riding in the lead so that another rider can come to the front.

Pusher: A rider who pedals in a large gear at a relatively slow cadence, relying on the gear size for speed.

Q

Quadriceps: The large muscle in front of the thigh, the strength of which helps determine a cyclist's ability to pedal with power.

R

Reach: The combined length of a bike's top tube and stem, which determines the rider's distance to the handlebar.

Rebound damping: How you control a shock during the return phase of its action.

Repetition: Each hard effort in an interval workout. Also, one complete movement in a weight training exercise. Rep for short.

Resistance trainer: A stationary training device into which the bike is clamped. Pedaling resistance increases with pedaling speed to simulate actual riding. Also known as an indoor, wind, or mag trainer (the last two names derived from the fan or magnet that creates resistance on the rear wheel).

Road race: A mass-start race on pavement that goes from point to point, covers one large loop, or is held on a circuit longer than those used for criteriums.

Rollers: An indoor training device consisting of three or four long cylinders connected by belts. Both bike wheels roll on these cylinders so that balancing is much like actual riding.

S

Saddle sore: Skin problem in the crotch that develops from chafing caused by pedaling action. Sores can range from tender raw spots to boil-like lesions if infection occurs.

Saddle time: Time spent cycling.

Sag wagon: A motor vehicle that follows a group of riders, carrying equipment and lending assistance in the event of difficulty. Also called the broom wagon.

Schrader: An inner tube valve identical to those found on car tires. A tiny plunger in the center of its opening must be depressed for air to enter or exit.

Set: In intervals or weight training, a specific number of repetitions.

Singletrack: A trail so narrow that two cyclists can't easily ride side by side, which makes passing difficult or impossible.

Sit on a wheel: To ride in someone's draft.

Slingshot: To ride up behind another rider with help from his draft, then use the momentum to sprint past.

Slipstream: The pocket of calmer air behind a moving rider. Also called the draft.

Snap: The ability to accelerate quickly.

Soft-pedal: To rotate the pedals without actually applying power.

Speed: The ability to accelerate quickly and maintain a very fast cadence for brief periods.

Speedwork: A general term for intervals and other high-velocity training, such as sprints, time trials, and motorpacing.

Spin: To pedal at high cadence.

Spinner: A rider who pedals in a moderate gear at a relatively fast cadence, relying on pedal rpm for speed.

Spinning: A type of training involving stationary trainers and repeated intervals.

Squirrel: A nervous or unstable rider who can't be trusted to maintain a steady line.

Stage race: A multiday event consisting of various types of races. The winner is the rider with the lowest elapsed time for all races (stages).

Straight block: A cassette with cogs that increase in size in one-tooth increments.

Suppleness: A quality of highly conditioned leg muscles that allows a rider to pedal at high cadence with smoothness and power. Also known by the French term *souplesse*.

T

Take a flyer: To suddenly sprint away from a group.

Team time trial (TTT): A race against the clock with two or more riders working together.

Tempo: Fast riding at a brisk cadence.

Throw the bike: A racing technique in which a rider thrusts the bike ahead of his or her body at the finish line, gaining several inches in hopes of winning a close sprint.

Time trial (TT): A race against the clock in which individual riders start at set intervals and cannot give or receive a draft.

Tops: The part of a drop handlebar between the stem and the brake levers.

Training effect: The result of exercise done with an intensity and duration sufficient to bring about positive physiological changes.

Travel: In suspensions, the maximum distance a fork or rear shock can compress.

Tubeless: A type of clincher tire in which the bead forms an airtight seal with the rim, eliminating the need for an inner tube. Allows mountain bike tires to be run at extremely low pressures, for increased traction.

Tubular: A lightweight tire that is glued to the wheel rim and has its tube sewn inside the casing. Also called a sew-up.

Turkey: An unskilled cyclist.

Turnaround: The point where the riders reverse direction on an out-and-back time trial course.

U

UCI: Union Cycliste Internationale, the world governing body of bicycle racing headquartered in Geneva, Switzerland. See www.uci.ch/english/#UCI.

Unweight: The act of momentarily lightening the bike through a combination of body movement and position. It's integral to techniques such as wheelies, bunnyhops, and jumps.

Upshift: To shift to a higher gear, that is, a smaller cog or a larger chainring.

USA Cycling: The umbrella organization for American bicycle racing. Affiliated with the UCI.

USCF: U.S. Cycling Federation, the organization that governs amateur road, cyclocross, and track racing in America. A division of USA Cycling. Visit www.ushf.org.

USPRO: U.S. Professional Racing Organization, the organization in charge of professional bicycle racing in America. A division of USA Cycling.

V

Velodrome: A banked track for bicycle racing.

W

Wheelie: To elevate the front wheel and ride on the rear wheel only. The opposite is called a nose wheelie.

Wheelsucker: Someone who drafts behind others but doesn't take a pull.

Windchill: The effect of air moving across the skin, making the temperature seem colder than it actually is. A cyclist creates a windchill even on a calm day, a situation that must be considered when dressing for winter rides.

Windup: Steady acceleration to an all-out effort.

INDEX

Boldface page references indicate photographs and illustrations. <u>Underscored</u> references indicate boxed text.